MORE ADVANCE PRAISE FOR
## DON'T THINK OF AN ELEPHANT!

"This is a pocket manifesto for those who still wonder how a small group of rich, powerful oligarchs tied together the shoelaces of the progressive movement. Read it once, and know why we are losing. Read it twice, and we can restore sanity to the world."

—Paul Hawken, coauthor of *Natural Capitalism*

"I learned a lot from Lakoff. You will too."

—George Soros

"*Don't Think of an Elephant!* is a work of genius. As George Lakoff explains how the right has framed the notion of the political center, he presents both the most original and the most practical analysis of United States politics in many years."

—George Akerlof, University of California, Berkeley, and Nobel Prize winner in Economics

"Are you tired of explaining to reporters why they shouldn't call Bush's clear-cut extravaganza 'healthy forests'? Does it bother you that the power plants upwind from your community will keep on poisoning you with mercury in the name of 'clear skies'? Do you wonder what 'family value' is advanced by shifting the cost of cleaning up toxic waste from polluters to victims?

"If you want to take back our country, you have to take back your community. If you want to take back your community, you need to take back the debate. This book, and the video that go with it, are your essential tools. What the Bush administration has done for obfuscation, George Lakoff's work does for clarification."

—Carl Pope, Executive Director, Sierra Club, and author of *Strategic Ignorance: Why the Bush Administration Is Recklessly Destroying a Century of Environmental Progresss*

"Progressives have a lot to learn about persuading swing voters to our cause, and there's no better teacher than George Lakoff. This readable text couldn't be more timely; it should be read widely and put to work!"

—Daniel Ellsberg, author of *Secrets: A Memoir of Vietnam and the Pentagon Papers*

"George Lakoff's *Don't Think of an Elephant!* is a wonderful example of what happens when you combine a linguist's ear for the subtleties of language with an understanding of the complexities of modern politics and a commitment to progressive ideals. Whether you think of yourself as a liberal, a progressive, or simply someone with an interest in how political language works, this is a must read."

—Geoffrey Nunberg, Consulting Professor of Linguistics, Stanford University, and author of *Going Nucular*

"Ever wonder how the radical right has been able to convince average Americans to repeatedly vote against their own interests? It's the framing, stupid! *Don't Think of an Elephant!* is a pithy and powerful primer on the language of American politics, and a vital reminder that he who creates the political framework controls the picture that's put inside. It's also a detailed roadmap out of the mess we are in. Lakoff shows how progressives can reclaim the political narrative—and, in the process, change our country and our world for the better."

—Arianna Huffington, syndicated columnist and author of *Fanatics & Fools: The Game Plan for Winning Back America*

"It's not enough that we have reason on our side. Lakoff offers crucial lessons in how to counter right-wing demagoguery. Essential reading in this neo-Orwellian age of Bush-speak."

—Robert B. Reich, Maurice Hexter Professor of Social and Economic Policy, Brandeis University, and author of *Reason: Why Liberals Will Win the Battle for America*

# DON'T THINK OF AN ELEPHANT!

## Other Books by George Lakoff

*Moral Politics: How Liberals and Conservatives Think*. Chicago: University of Chicago Press, 1996; 2nd ed., 2002.

*Metaphors We Live By* (with Mark Johnson). Chicago: University of Chicago Press, 1980; 2nd ed., 2003.

*Women, Fire, and Dangerous Things: What Categories Reveal About The Mind*. Chicago: University of Chicago Press, 1987.

*More Than Cool Reason: A Guide to Poetic Metaphor* (with Mark Turner). Chicago: University of Chicago Press, 1989.

*Philosophy in the Flesh: The Embodied Mind and Its Challenge to Western Thought* (with Mark Johnson). New York: Basic Books, 1999.

*Where Mathematics Comes From: How the Embodied Mind Brings Mathematics into Being* (with Rafael Núñez). New York: Basic Books, 2000.

# DON'T THINK OF AN ELEPHANT!

*Know Your Values and Frame the Debate*

## GEORGE LAKOFF

### THE ESSENTIAL GUIDE FOR PROGRESSIVES

Foreword by **HOWARD DEAN**
Introduction by **DON HAZEN**

CHELSEA GREEN PUBLISHING
WHITE RIVER JUNCTION, VERMONT

Managing Editor: Collette Leonard
Developmental Editor: Jennifer Nix
Project Editor: Marcy Brant
Copy Editor: Robin Catalano
Designer: Peter Holm
Design Assistant: Daria Hoak
Printed in Canada
First printing, September, 2004
10 9 8 7 6 5 4
Printed on acid-free, recycled paper

Library of Congress Cataloging-in-Publication Data
Lakoff, George.
Don't think of an elephant! : know your values and frame the debate : the
essential guide for progressives / by George Lakoff.
    p. cm.
Includes bibliographical references and index.
ISBN 1-931498-71-7 (pbk. : alk. paper)
  1. Communication in politics—United States. 2. Progressivism (United
States politics) 3. United States—Politics and government—2001- I.
Title.
JA85.2.U6L35 2004
320.51'3'0973--dc22
                                        2004018919

Chelsea Green Publishing Company
Post Office Box 428
White River Junction, VT 05001
(800) 639-4099
www.chelseagreen.com

The following chapters appeared earlier and are reprinted here with the author's
approval.
    Chapter 2 previously appeared as "The Frame Around Arnold," *AlterNet*, October
13, 2003. http://www.alternet.org/story.html?StoryID=16947.
    Chapter 3 previously appeared as "What's in a Word?" *AlterNet*, February 18,
2004. http://www.alternet.org/story.html?StoryID=17876.
    Chapter 4 previously appeared as "Metaphors of Terror," University of Chicago Press
Web site, September 16, 2001. http://www.press.uchicago.edu/News/911lakoff.html.
    Chapter 5 previously appeared as "Metaphor and War Again," *AlterNet*, March 18,
2003. http://www.alternet.org/story.html?StoryID=15414.
    Chapter 6 previously appeared as "Betrayal of Trust," *AlterNet*, September 15,
2003. http://www.alternet.org/story.html?StoryID=16771.

To
Kathleen, Andy, Ezra, and Hera

# CONTENTS

# FOREWORD

If only the Democrats had read George Lakoff a few years ago, we might not be in the position we find ourselves in today: out of power in the White House, out of power in Congress, and out of power in the Courts.

Lakoff has written down, in language liberals can understand, what Ralph Reed, Newt Gingrich, and Frank Luntz intuitively realized a long time ago. Language matters.

By defining a concept such as tax relief, the right wing of the Republican party not only set the terms of the debate, they seized the high ground. By defining tax cuts as tax relief, the right also defined those who were against tax cuts as essentially bad people.

If you are confused by this, you desperately need to read this book. Lakoff's insights will not only send a chill of recognition through you. More importantly, he shows us the way out of the morass. Americans who want to be first to set the agenda need to be quick, and must understand the use of language. Agenda setters also need to be unapologetic and unafraid.

George Lakoff will be one of the most influential political thinkers of the progressive movement when the history of this century is written. It is up to those who want change to make good use of his unique insights.

—HOWARD DEAN

The defeat of the Democrats in November of 2004 was a huge shock to many. Depression set in first, followed by a quick rebound. Millions of progressives wanted to know what happened and what they could do. Many realized that the same old tactic of simply targeting voters with a powerful anti-Bush message was not enough.

As polls dramatically underscored, many Americans voted their moral identity and values, often at the expense of their economic interests. But communicating about values is not something that Democrats have mastered. Overwhelming facts and statistics, debate victories, and proffered new policies did not translate into enough votes for a Kerry win. With the election behind us, it is even clearer that Lakoff's ideas are at the very core of the work we need to be doing—and now.

Progressives need to do the hard work of determining our values and reframing the political debate. We need to state those values and messages early and often. And for those who want to rethink and redo politics, there is no better place to start than with the book you now hold in your hands.

Not too long ago, George Lakoff was relatively unknown. He was admired in academic circles and favored by a small group of progressive and media insiders. But Lakoff was clearly a rarified taste; his ideas had not yet reached the people needed to create real change: progressives all across America.

Not anymore. George Lakoff is on the road to fame and renown, read and listened to by presidential and congressional candidates, leaders of major national groups, and increasingly, the average American. This book has brought Lakoff's ideas on the science and art of framing into the mainstream, as evidenced by its rapid climb onto bestseller lists around the country within weeks of its release. This, without any advertising budget!

And dear reader, if you care about social change, part of your job is to continue this "viral marketing" and help spread the ideas in this book. Buy ten more copies and give them out to friends, family, and allies in working for change. If we are serious about changing our country, if we are going to take it back from the right-wing fundamentalists, then this book is a great place to start. The struggle will continue. The right has a long head start, but we can catch up fast. And if we do it right, our lives will never be the same.

Lakoff's growing influence and acceptance has happened for several reasons. First, in 2000, we progressives and independents suddenly found ourselves in a nightmare. After the Supreme Court gave the election to George W. Bush, Republicans were in charge of virtually everything. But in our hearts we knew that their ideas were far out of the mainstream and things were totally out of whack. We found ourselves living in a country where what was considered extreme just a decade ago was now national policy. How could this have happened?

When we tried to figure out what had occurred, the one person who had the best explanation, who knew all along that the radical right-wing transformation was underway, was George Lakoff.

Lakoff provided the narrative that made the most sense and the research to back up his analysis. He reminded us how, over a period of forty years, the radical right and its rich patrons had invested many hundreds of millions of dollars in think tanks, young talent, spokespeople, and communications capacity that had essentially transformed the language of American politics. And when you control the language, you control the message, and the corporate media does the rest.

Lakoff knew as well as anyone how and why this transformation happened, and more importantly, what could be done about it. He took it upon himself to become the pied piper of media framing— how we have to be cognizant about how we communicate, the words we choose, and the framing we evoke, at all times.

Early adopters like Peter Teague at the Nathan Cummings

Foundation helped George Lakoff travel the country in 2002 and 2003 talking with thousands of activists and leaders and turning them on to the importance of framing. George started working with MoveOn.org and with major environmental groups. The SPIN Project was using framing in its trainings, while media outlets like AlterNet.org (where I am the executive editor), *The American Prospect,* and BuzzFlash showcased George's ideas. Before long, a "tipping point" was reached. Suddenly Lakoff was hot, but more importantly, thousands of people were thinking differently about communications and language.

We now understood how terms like *tax relief, partial birth abortion,* and *death tax* got invented by the right to invoke frames and dominate debates. Even our allies were using language invented by the conservatives, shooting themselves in the foot every time.

An important element of understanding framing is that you can learn a valuable aspect in thirty seconds. If nothing else, if we all can understand the lesson of "don't think of an elephant"—that attacking our opponents' frame reinforces their message—we will have taken a giant step forward. Our job is to frame our own values, vision, and mission, and avoid attacking theirs, because if we do, it only keeps their ideas in the forefront.

Progressives have been under the illusion that if only people understood the facts, we'd be fine. Wrong. The facts alone will not set us free. People make decisions about politics and candidates based on their value system, and the language and frames that invoke those values. Their values—strict authoritarian values in the conservatives' case—are what motivate them to enter the voting booth. Sadly, we saw this play out yet again in the 2004 election, with conservatives increasing their vote for the president and their control of both houses of Congress.

We need to start today if we are going to rebuild a more tolerant, secure, and truly free society.

With this book in your hands, you are part of a growing community of people who better understand how to move forward and communicate more effectively. But the book is just the first step. Language and framing is all about metaphor, and while the basic precepts are easy to grasp, reclaiming the language requires some serious thinking and lots of practice. But now you own the field guide. So get out there and start framing our messages and vision for the future.

—DON HAZEN, ALTERNET.ORG

## PREFACE

# Reframing *Is* Social Change

Frames are mental structures that shape the way we see the world. As a result, they shape the goals we seek, the plans we make, the way we act, and what counts as a good or bad outcome of our actions. In politics our frames shape our social policies and the institutions we form to carry out policies. To change our frames is to change all of this. Reframing *is* social change.

You can't see or hear frames. They are part of what cognitive scientists call the "cognitive unconscious"—structures in our brains that we cannot consciously access, but know by their consequences: the way we reason and what counts as common sense. We also know frames through language. All words are defined relative to conceptual frames. When you hear a word, its frame (or collection of frames) is activated in your brain.

Reframing is changing the way the public sees the world. It is changing what counts as common sense. Because language activates frames, new language is required for new frames. Thinking differently requires speaking differently.

At present, there is only one progressive think tank engaged in a major reframing enterprise: the Rockridge Institute (www.rock ridgeinstitute.org). It is new and growing. Rockridge brings together cognitive scientists and linguists with social scientists to reframe the full range of public policy issues from a progressive perspective. Rockridge research is nonpartisan and is published openly on its Web site. This book uses and extends that research.

It is by popular demand that this book is short and informal. It is meant to be a practical guide both for citizen activists and for anyone with a serious interest in politics. Those who want a more systematic and scholarly treatment should read my book *Moral Politics: How Liberals and Conservatives Think* (second edition).

This book was written and published in time for the 2004 election. But it has become even more important since then. The exit polls revealed what this book predicted, that moral values were more important than any particular issue—more important than terrorism, the war, the economy, health care, or education. Progressives came together in that election like never before in recent history. What united them in their gut, what told them that Bush was immoral, was their own progressive values.

It is vital—for us, for our country, and for the world—that we stay united. It is our values that unite us. We must learn to articulate those values loud and clear. If the Democrats are to win in the future, the party must present a clear moral vision to the country—a moral vision common to all progressives. It cannot just present a laundry list of programs. It must present a moral alternative, one more traditionally American, one that lies behind everything Americans are proud of.

This book is written in the service of that vision.

Enjoy!

—GEORGE LAKOFF
NOVEMBER 2004

# PART ONE

# THEORY AND APPLICATION

# Framing 101: How to Take Back Public Discourse

— JANUARY 21, 2004 —

On this date I spoke extemporaneously to a group of about two hundred progressive citizen-activists in Sausalito, California.

When I teach the study of framing at Berkeley, in Cognitive Science 101, the first thing I do is I give my students an exercise. The exercise is: Don't think of an elephant! Whatever you do, do *not* think of an elephant. I've never found a student who is able to do this. Every word, like *elephant*, evokes a frame, which can be an image or other kinds of knowledge: Elephants are large, have floppy ears and a trunk, are associated with circuses, and so on. The word is defined relative to that frame. When we negate a frame, we evoke the frame.

Richard Nixon found that out the hard way. While under pressure to resign during the Watergate scandal, Nixon addressed the nation on TV. He stood before the nation and said, "I am not a crook." And everybody thought about him as a crook.

This gives us a basic principle of framing, for when you are arguing against the other side: Do not use their language. Their language picks out a frame—and it won't be the frame you want.

Let me give you an example. On the day that George W. Bush arrived in the White House, the phrase *tax relief* started coming out of the White House. It still is: It was used a number of times in this year's State of the Union address, and is showing up more and more in preelection speeches four years later.

Think of the framing for *relief*. For there to be relief there must be an affliction, an afflicted party, and a reliever who removes the affliction and is therefore a hero. And if people try to stop the hero, those people are villains for trying to prevent relief.

When the word *tax* is added to *relief*, the result is a metaphor: Taxation is an affliction. And the person who takes it away is a hero, and anyone who tries to stop him is a bad guy. This is a frame. It is made up of ideas, like *affliction* and *hero*. The language that evokes the frame comes out of the White House, and it goes into press releases, goes to every radio station, every TV station, every newspaper. And soon the *New York Times* is using *tax relief*. And it is not only on Fox; it is on CNN, it is on NBC, it is on every station because it is "the president's tax-relief plan." And soon the Democrats are using *tax relief*—and shooting themselves in the foot.

It is remarkable. I was asked by the Democratic senators to visit their caucus just before the president's tax plan was to come up in the Senate. They had their version of the tax plan, and it was their version of tax relief. They were accepting the conservative frame. The conservatives had set a trap: The words draw you into *their* worldview.

That is what framing is about. Framing is about getting language that fits your worldview. It is not just language. The ideas are primary—and the language carries those ideas, evokes those ideas.

There was another good example in the State of the Union address in January. This one was a remarkable metaphor to find in a State of the Union address. Bush said, "We do not need a permission slip to defend America." What is going on with a *permission slip*? He could have just said, "We won't ask permission." But talking about a permission slip is different. Think about when you last needed a permission slip. Think about who has to ask for a permission slip. Think about who is being asked. Think about the relationship between them.

Those are the kinds of questions you need to ask if you are to understand contemporary political discourse. While you are contemplating them, I want to raise other questions for you.

My work on politics began when I asked myself just such a question. It was back in the fall of 1994. I was watching election speeches and reading the Republicans' "Contract with America." The question I asked myself was this: What do the conservatives' positions on issues have to do with each other? If you are a conservative, what does your position on abortion have to do with your position on taxation? What does that have to do with your position on the environment? Or foreign policy? How do these positions fit together? What does being against gun control have to do with being for tort reform? What makes sense of the linkage? I could not figure it out. I said to myself, *These are strange people. Their collection of positions makes no sense.* But then an embarrassing thought occurred to me. *I have exactly the opposite position on every issue. What do my positions have to do with one another?* And I could not figure that out either.

That was extremely embarrassing for someone who does cognitive science and linguistics.

Eventually the answer came. And it came from a very unexpected place. It came from the study of family values. I had asked myself why conservatives were talking so much about family values. And why did certain values count as "family values" while others did not? Why would anyone in a presidential campaign, in congressional campaigns, and so on, when the future of the world was being threatened by nuclear proliferation and global warming, constantly talk about family values?

At this point I remembered a paper that one of my students had written some years back that showed that we all have a metaphor for the nation as a family. We have Founding Fathers. The Daughters of the American Revolution. We "send our sons" to war. This is a natural metaphor because we usually understand large social groups, like nations, in terms of small ones, like families or communities.

Given the existence of the metaphor linking the nation to the family, I asked the next question: If there are two different understandings of the nation, do they come from two different understandings of family?

I worked backward. I took the various positions on the conservative side and on the progressive side and I said, "Let's put them through the metaphor from the opposite direction and see what comes out." I put in the two different views of the nation, and out popped two different models of the family: a strict father family and a nurturant parent family. You know which is which.

Now, when I first did this—and I'll tell you about the details in a minute—I was asked to give a talk at a linguistics convention. I decided I would talk about this discovery. In the audience were two members of the Christian Coalition who were linguists and good friends of mine. Excellent linguists. And very, very good people. Very nice people. People I liked a lot. They took me aside at the party afterward and said, "Well, this strict father model of the family, it's close, but not quite right. We'll help you get the details right. However, you should know all this. Have you read Dobson?"

I said, "Who?"

They said, "*James* Dobson."

I said, "*Who?*"

They said, "You're kidding. He's on three thousand radio stations."

I said, "Well, I don't think he's on NPR. I haven't heard of him."

They said, "Well, you live in Berkeley."

"Where would I . . . does he write stuff?"

"Oh," they said, "oh yes. He has sold millions of books. His classic is *Dare to Discipline.*"

My friends were right. I followed their directions to my local Christian bookstore, and there I found it all laid out: the strict father model in all its details. Dobson not only has a 100-to-200-million-dollar-a-year operation, but he also has his own ZIP code, so many people are writing to order his books and pamphlets. He is teaching people how to use the strict father model to raise their kids, and he understands its connection to right-wing politics.

The strict father model begins with a set of assumptions:

*The world is a dangerous place, and it always will be, because there is evil out there in the world. The world is also difficult because it is competitive. There will always be winners and losers. There is an absolute right and an absolute wrong. Children are born bad, in the sense that they just want to do what feels good, not what is right. Therefore, they have to be made good.*

*What is needed in this kind of a world is a strong, strict father who can:*

- *Protect the family in the dangerous world,*
- *Support the family in the difficult world, and*
- *Teach his children right from wrong.*

*What is required of the child is obedience, because the strict father is a moral authority who knows right from wrong. It is further assumed that the only way to teach kids obedience—that is, right from wrong— is through punishment, painful punishment, when they do wrong. This includes hitting them, and some authors on conservative child rearing recommend sticks, belts, and wooden paddles on the bare bottom. Some authors suggest this start at birth, but Dobson is more liberal. "There is no excuse for spanking babies younger than fifteen or eighteen months of age" (Dobson,* The New Dare to Discipline, *65).*

*The rationale behind physical punishment is this: When children do something wrong, if they are physically disciplined they learn not to do it again. That means that they will develop internal discipline to keep themselves from doing wrong, so that in the future they will be obedient and act morally. Without such punishment, the world will go to hell. There will be no morality.*

*Such internal discipline has a secondary effect. It is what is required for success in the difficult, competitive world. That is, if people are disciplined and pursue their self-interest in this land of opportunity, they will become prosperous and self-reliant. Thus, the strict father model links morality with prosperity. The same discipline you need to be moral is what allows you to prosper. The link is the pursuit of self-interest.*

*Given opportunity and discipline, pursuing your self-interest should enable you to prosper.*

Now, Dobson is very clear about the connection between the strict father worldview and free market capitalism. The link is the morality of self-interest, which is a version of Adam Smith's view of capitalism. Adam Smith said that if everyone pursues their own profit, then the profit of all will be maximized by the invisible hand—that is, by nature—just naturally. Go about pursuing your own profit, and you are helping everyone.

This is linked to a general metaphor that views well-being as wealth. For example, if I do you a favor, you say, "I owe you one" or "I'm in your debt." Doing something good for someone is metaphorically like giving him money. He "owes" you something. And he says, "How can I ever repay you?"

Applying this metaphor to Adam Smith's "law of nature," if everyone pursues her own self-interest, then by the invisible hand, by nature, the self-interest of all will be maximized. That is, it is moral to pursue your self-interest, and there is a name for those people who do not do it. The name is do-gooder. A do-gooder is someone who is trying to help someone else rather than herself and is getting in the way of those who are pursuing their self-interest. Do-gooders screw up the system.

In this model there is also a definition of what it means to become a good person. A good person—a moral person—is someone who is disciplined enough to be obedient, to learn what is right, do what is right and not do what is wrong, and to pursue her self-interest to prosper and become self-reliant. A good child grows up to be like that. A bad child is one who does not learn discipline, does not function morally, does not do what is right, and therefore is not disciplined enough to become prosperous. She cannot take care of herself and thus becomes dependent.

When the good children are mature, they either have learned discipline and can prosper, or have failed to learn it. From this point on the strict father is not to meddle in their lives. This translates politically into no government meddling.

Consider what all this means for social programs. It is immoral to give people things they have not earned, because then they will not develop discipline and will become both dependent and immoral. This theory says that social programs are immoral because they make people dependent. Promoting social programs is immoral. And what does this say about budgets? Well, if there are a lot of progressives in Congress who think that there should be social programs, and if you believe that social programs are immoral, how do you stop these immoral people?

It is quite simple. What you have to do is reward the good people—the ones whose prosperity reveals their discipline and hence their capacity for morality—with a tax cut, and make it big enough so that there is not enough money left for social programs. By this logic, the deficit is a *good* thing. As Grover Norquist says, it "starves the beast."

Where liberals and fiscal conservatives take Bush's huge deficit as bad, right-wing radicals following strict father morality see it as good. In the State of the Union address in January 2004, the president said that he thinks they can cut the deficit in half by cutting out "wasteful spending"—that is, spending for "bad" social programs. Are conservatives against all government? No. They are not against the military, they are not against homeland defense, they are not against the current Department of Justice, nor against the courts, nor the Departments of Treasury and Commerce. There are many aspects of government that they like very much. They are not against government subsidies for industry. Subsidies for corporations, which reward the good people—the investors in those corporations—are great. No problem there.

But they are against nurturance and care. They are against social programs that take care of people. That is what they see as wrong. That is what they are trying to eliminate on moral grounds. That is why they are not merely a bunch of crazies or mean and greedy—or stupid—people, as many liberals believe. What is even scarier is that conservatives believe it. They believe it is moral. And they have supporters around the country. People who have strict father morality and who apply it to politics are going to believe that this is the right way to govern.

Think for a minute about what this says about foreign policy. Suppose you are a moral authority. As a moral authority, how do you deal with your children? Do you ask them what they should do or what you should do? No. You tell them. What the father says, the child does. No back talk. Communication is one-way. It is the same with the White House. That is, the president does not ask; the president tells. If you are a moral authority you know what is right, you have power, and you use it. You would be immoral yourself if you abandoned your moral authority.

Map this onto foreign policy, and it says that you cannot give up sovereignty. The United States, being the best and most powerful country in the world—a moral authority—knows the right thing to do. We should not be asking anybody else.

This belief comes together with a set of metaphors that have run foreign policy for a long time. There is a common metaphor learned in graduate school classes on international relations. It is called the rational actor metaphor. It is the basis of most international relations theory, and in turn it assumes another metaphor: that every nation is a person. Therefore there are "rogue states," there are "friendly nations," and so on. And there is a national interest.

What does it mean to act in your self-interest? In the most basic sense it means that you act in ways that will help you be healthy and strong. In the same way, by the metaphor that a nation is a person, it is good for a nation to be healthy (that is, economically healthy—defined as having a large GDP) and strong (that is, militarily strong). It is not necessary that all the individuals in the country be healthy, but the companies should be, and the country as a whole should have a lot of money. That is the idea.

The question is, How do you maximize your self-interest? That is what foreign policy is about: maximizing self-interest. The rational actor metaphor says that every actor, every person, is rational, and that it is irrational to act against your self-interest.

Therefore it is rational for every person to act to maximize self-interest. Then by the further metaphor that nations are persons ("friendly nations," "rogue states," "enemy nations," and so on), there are adult nations and child nations, where adulthood is industrialization. The child nations are called "developing" nations or "underdeveloped" states. Those are the backward ones. And what should we do? If you are a strict father, you tell the children how to develop, tell them what rules they should follow, and punish them when they do wrong. That is, you operate using, say, the policies of the International Monetary Fund.

And who is in the United Nations? Most of the United Nations consists of developing and underdeveloped countries. That means they are metaphorical children. Now let's go back to the State of the Union address. Should the United States have consulted the United Nations and gotten its permission to invade Iraq? An adult does not "ask for a permission slip"! The phrase itself, *permission slip*, puts you back in grammar school or high school, where you need a permission slip from an adult to go to the bathroom. You do not need to ask for a permission slip if you are the teacher, if you are the principal, if you are the person in power, the moral authority. The others should be asking *you* for permission. That is what the *permission slip* phrase in the 2004 State of the Union address was about. Every conservative in the audience got it. They got it right away.

Two powerful words: *permission slip*. What Bush did was evoke the adult-child metaphor for other nations. He said, "We're the adult." He was operating in the strict father worldview, and it did not have to be explained. It is evoked automatically. This is what is done regularly by the conservatives.

Now let me talk a bit about how progressives understand *their* morality and what their moral system is. It too comes out of a family model, what I call the nurturant parent model. The strict father worldview is so named because according to its own beliefs, the father is the head of the family. The nurturant parent worldview is gender neutral.

*Both parents are equally responsible for raising the children. The assumption is that children are born good and can be made better. The world can be made a better place, and our job is to work on that. The parents' job is to nurture their children and to raise their children to be nurturers of others.*

*What does nurturance mean? It means two things: empathy and responsibility. If you have a child, you have to know what every cry means. You have to know when the child is hungry, when he needs a diaper change, when he is having nightmares. And you have a responsibility—you have to take care of this child. Since you cannot take care of someone else if you are not taking care of yourself, you have to take care of yourself enough to be able to take care of the child.*

*All this is not easy. Anyone who has ever raised a child knows that this is hard. You have to be strong. You have to work hard at it. You have to be very competent. You have to know a lot.*

*In addition, all sorts of other values immediately follow from empathy and responsibility. Think about it.*

*First, if you empathize with your child, you will provide protection. This comes into politics in many ways. What do you protect your child from? Crime and drugs, certainly. You also protect your child from cars without seat belts, from smoking, from poisonous additives in food. So progressive politics focuses on environmental protection, worker protection, consumer protection, and protection from disease. These are the things that progressives want the government to protect their citizens from. But there are also terrorist attacks, which liberals and progressives have not been very good at talking about in terms of protection. Protection is part of the progressive moral system, but it has not been elaborated on enough. And on September 11, progressives did not have a whole lot to say. That was unfortunate, because nurturant parents and progressives do care about protection. Protection is important. It is part of our moral system.*

*Second, if you empathize with your child, you want your child to be fulfilled in life, to be a happy person. And if you are an unhappy, unfulfilled person yourself, you are not going to want other people to be hap-*

*pier than you are. The Dalai Lama teaches us that. Therefore it is your moral responsibility to be a happy, fulfilled person. Your moral responsibility. Further, it is your moral responsibility to teach your child to be a happy, fulfilled person who wants others to be happy and fulfilled. That is part of what nurturing family life is about. It is a common precondition for caring about others.*

*There are still other nurturant values.*

- *If you want your child to be fulfilled in life, the child has to be free enough to do that. Therefore **freedom** is a value.*
- *You do not have very much freedom if there is no opportunity or prosperity. Therefore **opportunity** and **prosperity** are progressive values.*
- *If you really care about your child, you want your child to be treated fairly by you and by others. Therefore **fairness** is a value.*
- *If you are connecting with your child and you empathize with that child, you have to have **open, two-way communication**. Honest communication. That becomes a value.*
- *You live in a community, and that the community will affect how your child grows up. Therefore **community-building, service to the community,** and **cooperation in a community** become values.*
- *To have cooperation, you must have **trust**, and to have trust you must have **honesty** and **open two-way communication**. Trust, honesty, and open communication are fundamental progressive values—in a community as in a family.*

These are the nurturant values—and they are the progressive values. As progressives, you all have them. You know you have them. You recognize them.

Every progressive political program is based on one or more of these values. That is what it means to be a progressive.

There are several types of progressives. How many types? I am asking as a cognitive scientist, not as a sociologist or a political scientist. From the point of view of a cognitive scientist, who looks at modes of thought, there are six basic types of progressives, each with a distinct mode of thought. They share all the progressive values, but are distinguished by some differences.

1. **Socioeconomic progressives** think that everything is a matter of money and class and that all solutions are ultimately economic and social class solutions.
2. **Identity politics progressives** say it is time for their oppressed group to get its share now.
3. **Environmentalists** think in terms of sustainability of the earth, the sacredness of the earth, and the protection of native peoples.
4. **Civil liberties progressives** want to maintain freedoms against threats to freedom.
5. **Spiritual progressives** have a nurturant form of religion or spirituality, their spiritual experience has to do with their connection to other people and the world, and their spiritual practice has to do with service to other people and to their community. Spiritual progressives span the full range from Catholics and Protestants to Jews, Muslims, Buddhists, Goddess worshippers, and pagan members of Wicca.
6. **Antiauthoritarians** say there are all sorts of illegitimate forms of authority out there and we have to fight them, whether they are big corporations or anyone else.

All six types are examples of nurturant parent morality. The problem is that many of the people who have one of these modes of thought do not recognize that theirs is just one special case of something more general, and do not see the unity in all the types of progressives. They often think that theirs is the only way to be a true progressive. That is sad. It keeps people who share progressive values from coming together. We have to get past that harmful idea. The other side did.

Back in the 1950s conservatives hated each other. The financial conservatives hated the social conservatives. The libertarians did not get along with the social conservatives or the religious conservatives. And many social conservatives were not religious. A group of conservative leaders got together around William F. Buckley Jr. and others and started asking what the different groups of conservatives had in common and whether they could agree to disagree in order to promote a general conservative cause. They started magazines and think tanks, and invested billions of dollars. The first thing they did, their first victory, was getting Barry Goldwater nominated in 1964. He lost, but when he lost they went back to the drawing board and put more money into organization.

During the Vietnam War, they noticed that most of the bright young people in the country were not becoming conservatives. *Conservative* was a dirty word. Therefore in 1970, Lewis Powell, just two months before he became a Supreme Court justice appointed by Nixon (at the time he was the chief counsel to the U.S. Chamber of Commerce), wrote a memo—the Powell memo (http://reclaimdemocracy.org/corporate_accountability/powell_m emo_lewis.html). It was a fateful document. He said that the conservatives had to keep the country's best and brightest young people from becoming antibusiness. What we need to do, Powell said, is set up institutes within the universities and outside the universities. We have to do research, we have to write books, we have to endow professorships to teach these people the right way to think.

After Powell went to the Supreme Court, these ideas were taken up by William Simon, the father of the present William Simon. At the time the elder Simon was secretary of the treasury under Nixon. He convinced some very wealthy people—Coors, Scaife,

Olin—to set up the Heritage Foundation, the Olin professorships, the Olin Institute at Harvard, and other institutions. These institutes have done their job very well. People associated with them have written more books than the people on the left have, on all issues. The conservatives support their intellectuals. They create media opportunities. They have media studios down the hall in institutes so that getting on television is easy. Eighty percent of the talking heads on television are from the conservative think tanks. Eighty percent.

When the amount of research money spent by the right over a period of time is compared with the amount of media time during that period, we see a direct correlation. In 2002 four times as much money was spent on research by the right as by the left, and they got four times as much media time. They get what they pay for.

This is not an accident. Conservatives, through their think tanks, figured out the importance of framing, and they figured out how to frame every issue. They figured out how to get those frames out there, how to get their people in the media all the time. They figured out how to bring their people together. Every Wednesday, Grover Norquist has a group meeting—around eighty people—of leaders from the full range of the right. They are invited, and they debate. They work out their differences, agree to disagree, and when they disagree, they trade off. The idea is, *This week he'll win on his issue. Next week, I'll win on mine.* Each one may not get everything he wants, but over the long haul, he gets a lot of what he wants.

Nothing like this happens in the progressive world, because there are so many people thinking that what each does is *the* right thing. It is not smart. It is self-defeating.

And what is worse is a set of myths believed by liberals and progressives. These myths come from a good source, but they end up hurting us badly.

The myths began with the Enlightenment, and the first one goes like this:

*The truth will set us free. If we just tell people the facts, since people are basically rational beings, they'll all reach the right conclusions.*

But we know from cognitive science that people do not think like that. People think in frames. The strict father and nurturing parent frames each force a certain logic. To be accepted, the truth must fit people's frames. If the facts do not fit a frame, the frame stays and the facts bounce off. Why?

Neuroscience tells us that each of the concepts we have—the long-term concepts that structure how we think—is instantiated in the synapses of our brains. Concepts are not things that can be changed just by someone telling us a fact. We may be presented with facts, but for us to make sense of them, they have to fit what is already in the synapses of the brain. Otherwise facts go in and then they go right back out. They are not heard, or they are not accepted as facts, or they mystify us: Why would anyone have said that? Then we label the fact as irrational, crazy, or stupid. That's what happens when progressives just "confront conservatives with the facts." It has little or no effect, unless the conservatives have a frame that makes sense of the facts.

Similarly, a lot of progressives hear conservatives talk and do not understand them because they do not have the conservatives' frames. They assume that conservatives are stupid.

They are not stupid. They are winning because they are smart. They understand how people think and how people talk. They think! That is what those think tanks are about. They support their intellectuals. They write all those books. They put their ideas out in public.

There are certainly cases where conservatives have lied. That is true. Of course, it is not true that *only* conservatives lie. But it is true that there are significant lies—even daily lies—by the Bush administration.

However, it is equally important to recognize that many of the ideas that outrage progressives are what conservatives see as truths—presented from their point of view. We must distinguish cases of out-and-out distortion, lying, and so on, from cases where conservatives are presenting what they consider truth.

Is it useful to go and tell everyone what the lies are? It is not useless or harmful for us to know when they are lying. But also remember that the truth alone will not set you free. Saying "the president lied when he started this war" puts the truth out there— but for many people it just bounces off. A huge number of people in the country still believe that Saddam Hussein was behind September 11. There are people who will believe this because it fits their understanding of the world. It fits their worldview. Given that, it is appropriate for them to believe. They still believe that Saddam Hussein and Al-Qaeda are the same thing, and that by fighting the war in Iraq we are protecting the country from terrorism. They believe this—in spite of the report by the 9/11 Commission. It is not that they are stupid. They have a frame and they only accept facts that fit that frame.

There is another myth that also comes from the Enlightenment, and it goes like this. It is irrational to go against your self-interest, and therefore a normal person, who is rational, reasons on the basis of self-interest. Modern economic theory and foreign policy are set up on the basis of that assumption.

The myth has been challenged by cognitive scientists such as Daniel Kahneman (who won the Nobel Prize in economics for his theory) and Amos Tversky, who have shown that people do not really think that way. Nevertheless, most of economics is still based on the assumption that people will naturally always think in terms of their self-interest.

This view of rationality comes into Democratic politics in a very important way. It is assumed that voters will vote their self-interest. Democrats are shocked or puzzled when voters do not vote their self-interest. "How," Democrats keep asking me, "can any poor person vote for Bush when he hurts them so badly?" Their response is to try to explain once more to the poor why voting Democratic would serve their self-interest. Despite all evidence to the contrary, Democrats keep banging their heads against the wall. In the 2000 election Gore kept saying that Bush's tax cuts would go only to the top 1 percent, and he thought that everyone else would follow their self-interest and support him. But poor conservatives still opposed him, because as conservatives they believed that those who had the most money—the "good" people—deserved to keep it as their reward for being disciplined. The bottom 99 percent of conservatives voted their conservative values, against their self-interest.

It is claimed that 35 percent of the populace thinks that they are, or someday will be, in the top 1 percent, and that this explains the finding on the basis of a hoped-for future self-interest. But what about the other 65 percent, who have no dream that they will ever get that tax cut but still support it? They are clearly not voting in their self-interest, or even their hoped-for future self-interest.

A similar phenomenon happened in the 2003 California recall election. Labor unions invested a lot of money presenting facts that Gray Davis's positions were better for people, especially for working people, than Arnold Schwarzenegger's. In focus groups, they asked union members, "Which is better for you, this Davis position or that Schwarzenegger position?" Most would say, "The Davis one." Davis, Davis, Davis. Then they would ask, "Who you voting for?" "Schwarzenegger."

People do not necessarily vote in their self-interest. They vote their identity. They vote their values. They vote for who they identify with. They may identify with their self-interest. That can happen. It is not that people never care about their self-interest. But they vote their identity. And if their identity fits their self-interest, they will vote for that. It is important to understand this point. It is a serious mistake to assume that people are simply always voting in their self-interest.

A third mistake is this: There is a metaphor that political campaigns are marketing campaigns where the candidate is the product and the candidate's positions on issues are the features and qualities of the product. This leads to the conclusion that polling should determine which issues a candidate should run on. Here's a list of issues. Which show the highest degree of support for a candidate's position? If it's prescription drugs, 78 percent, you run on a platform featuring prescription drugs. Is it keeping social security? You run on a platform featuring social security. You make a list of the top issues, and those are the issues you run on. You also do market segmentation: District by district, you find out the most important issues, and those are the ones you talk about when you go to that district.

It does not work. Sometimes it can be useful, and, in fact, the Republicans use it in addition to their real practice. But their real practice, and the real reason for their success, is this: They say what they idealistically believe. They say it; they talk to their base using the frames of their base. Liberal and progressive candidates tend to follow their polls and decide that they have to become more "centrist" by moving to the right. The conservatives do not move at all to the left, and yet they win!

Why? What is the electorate like from a cognitive point of view? Probably 35 to 40 percent of people—maybe more these days—have a strict father model governing their politics. Similarly, there are people who have a nurturant view governing their politics, probably another 35 to 40 percent. And then there are all the people in the "middle."

Notice that I said *governing* their politics. We all have both models, either actively or passively. Progressives see a John Wayne movie or an Arnold Schwarzenegger movie, and they can understand it. They do not say, "I don't know what's going on in this movie." They have a strict father model, at least passively. And if you are a conservative and you understand *The Cosby Show*, you have a nurturing parent model, at least passively. Everyone has both worldviews because both worldviews are widely present in our culture, but people do not necessarily live by one worldview all of the time.

So the question is, Are you living by one of the family-based models? But that question is not specific enough. There are many aspects of life, and many people live by one family-based model in one part of their lives and another in another part of their lives. I have colleagues who are nurturant parents at home and liberals in their politics, but strict fathers in their classrooms. Reagan knew that blue-collar workers who were nurturant in their union politics were often strict fathers at home. He used political metaphors that were based on the home and family, and got them to extend their strict father way of thinking from the home to politics.

This is very important to do. The goal is to activate *your* model in the people in the "middle." The people who are in the middle have *both* models, used regularly in different parts of their lives. What you want to do is to get them to use your model for politics—to activate your worldview and moral system in their political decisions. You do that by talking to people using frames based on your worldview.

However, in doing that, you do not want to offend the people in the middle who have up to this point made the opposite choice. Since they also have and use both models in some part of their lives, they might still be persuaded to activate the opposite model for politics.

Clinton figured out how to handle this problem. He stole the other side's language. He talked about "welfare reform," for example. He said, "The age of big government is over." He did what he wanted to do, only he took their language and used their words to describe it. It made them very mad. Very smart technique.

It turns out that what is good for the goose is good for the gander, and guess what? We get "compassionate conservatism." The Clear Skies Initiative. Healthy Forests. No Child Left Behind. This is the use of language to mollify people who have nurturant values, while the real policies are strict father policies. This mollifies, even attracts, the people in the middle who might have qualms about you. This is the use of Orwellian language—language that means the opposite of what it says—to appease people in the middle at the same time as you pump up the base. That is part of the conservative strategy.

Liberals and progressives typically react to this strategy in a self-defeating way. The usual reaction is, "Those conservatives are bad people; they are using Orwellian language. They are saying the opposite of what they mean. They are deceivers. Bad. Bad. "

All true. But we should recognize that they use Orwellian language precisely when they have to: when they are weak, when they cannot just come out and say what they mean. Imagine if they came out supporting a "Dirty Skies Bill" or a "Forest Destruction Bill" or a "Kill Public Education" bill. They would lose. They are aware people do not support what they are really trying to do.

Orwellian language points to weakness—Orwellian weakness. When you hear Orwellian language, note where it is, because it is a guide to where they are vulnerable. They do not use it everywhere. It is very important to notice this, and use their weakness to your advantage.

A very good example relates to the environment. The right's language man is Frank Luntz, who puts out big books of language guidelines for conservatives only, which are used as training manuals for all conservative candidates, as well as lawyers, judges, and other public speakers—even high school students who want to be conservative public figures. In these books, Luntz tells you what language to use.

For example, in last year's edition, the section on global warming says that science seems increasingly to be going against the conservative position. However, conservatives can counter the science using right language. People who support environmentalist positions like certain words. They like the words *healthy*, *clean*, and *safe* because these words fit frames that describe what the environment means to them. Therefore, Luntz says, use the words *healthy*, *clean*, and *safe* whenever possible, even when talking about coal plants or nuclear power plants. It is this kind of Orwellian weakness that causes a piece of legislation that actually increases pollution to be called the Clear Skies Act.

Similarly, a few years ago Luntz wrote a memo for talking to women. How do you talk to women? According to Luntz, women like certain words, so when you are talking to an audience of women, here are the words you use as many times as possible: *love, from the heart*, and *for the children*. And if you read Bush's speeches, *love, from the heart*, and *for the children* show up over and over again.

This kind of language use is a science. Like any science it can be used honestly or harmfully. This kind of language use is taught. This kind of language use is also a discipline. Conservatives enforce message discipline. In many offices there is a pizza fund: Every time you use the "wrong" language, you have to put a quarter in the pizza fund. People quickly learn to say *tax relief* or *partial-birth abortion*, not something else.

But Luntz is about much more than language. He recognizes that the right use of language starts with ideas—with the right framing of the issues, a framing that reflects a consistent conservative moral perspective, what we have called strict father morality. Luntz's book is not just about language. For each issue, he explains what the conservative reasoning is, what the progressive reasoning is, and how the progressive arguments can be best attacked from a conservative perspective. He is clear: Ideas come first.

One of the major mistakes liberals make is that they think they have all the ideas they need. They think that all they lack is media access. Or maybe some magic bullet phrases, like *partial-birth abortion*.

When you think you just lack words, what you really lack are ideas. Ideas come in the form of frames. When the frames are there, the words come readily. There's a way you can tell when you lack the right frames. There's a phenomenon you have probably noticed. A conservative on TV uses two words, like *tax relief*. And the progressive has to go into a paragraph-long discussion of his own view. The conservative can appeal to an established frame, that taxation is an affliction or burden, which allows for the two-word phrase *tax relief*. But there is no established frame on the other side. You can talk about it, but it takes some doing because there is no established frame, no fixed idea already out there.

In cognitive science there is a name for this phenomenon. It's called *hypocognition*—the lack of the ideas you need, the lack of a relatively simple fixed frame that can be evoked by a word or two.

The idea of hypocognition comes from a study in Tahiti in the 1950s by the late anthropologist Bob Levy, who was also a therapist. Levy addressed the question of why there were so many suicides in Tahiti, and discovered that Tahitians did not have a concept of grief. They felt grief. They experienced it. But they did not have a concept for it or a name for it. They did not see it as a normal emotion. There were no rituals around grief. No grief counseling, nothing like it. They lacked a concept they needed—and wound up committing suicide all too often.

Progressives are suffering from massive hypocognition. The conservatives used to suffer from it. When Goldwater lost in 1964, they had very few of the concepts that they have today. In the intermediate forty years, conservative thinkers have filled in their conceptual gaps. But our conceptual gaps are still there.

Let's go back to *tax relief*.

What is taxation? Taxation is what you pay to live in a civilized country—what you pay to have democracy and opportunity, and what you pay to use the infrastructure paid for by previous taxpayers: the highway system, the Internet, the entire scientific establishment, the medical establishment, the communications system, the airline system. All are paid for by taxpayers.

You can think of it metaphorically in at least two ways. First, as an investment. Imagine the following ad:

Our parents invested in the future, ours as well as theirs, through their taxes. They invested their tax money in the interstate highway system, the Internet, the scientific and medical establishments, our communications system, our airline system, the space program. They invested in the future, and we are reaping the tax benefits, the benefits from the taxes they paid. Today we have assets—highways, schools and colleges, the Internet, airlines—that come from the wise investments they made.

Imagine versions of this ad running over and over, for years. Eventually, the frame would be established: Taxes are wise investments in the future.

Or take another metaphor:

Taxation is paying your dues, paying your membership fee in America. If you join a country club or a community center, you pay fees. Why? You did not build the swimming pool. You have to maintain it. You did not build the basketball court. Someone has to clean it. You may not use the squash court, but you still have to pay your dues. Otherwise it won't be maintained and will fall apart. People who avoid taxes, like corporations that move to Bermuda, are not paying their dues to their country. It is patriotic to be a taxpayer. It is traitorous to desert our country and not pay your dues.

Perhaps Bill Gates Sr. said it best. In arguing to keep the inheritance tax, he pointed out that he and Bill Jr. did not invent the Internet. They just used it—to make billions. There is no such thing as a self-made man. Every businessman has used the vast American infrastructure, which the taxpayers

paid for, to make his money. He did not make his
money alone. He used taxpayer infrastructure. He
got rich on what other taxpayers had paid for: the
banking system, the Federal Reserve, the Treasury
and Commerce Departments, and the judicial
system, where nine-tenths of cases involve corporate law. These taxpayer investments support companies and wealthy investors. There are no
self-made men! The wealthy have gotten rich using
what previous taxpayers have paid for. They owe
the taxpayers of this country a great deal and should
be paying it back.

These are accurate views of taxes, but they are not yet enshrined
in our brains. They need to be repeated over and over again, and
refined until they take their rightful place in our synapses. But
that takes time. It does not happen overnight. Start now.

It is not an accident that conservatives are winning where they
have successfully framed the issues. They've got a thirty- to forty-
year head start. And more than two billion dollars in think tank
investments.

And they are still thinking ahead. Progressives are not.
Progressives feel so assaulted by conservatives that they can only
think about immediate defense. Democratic office holders are
constantly under attack. Every day they have to respond to conservative initiatives. It is always, "What do we have to do to
fight them off today?" It leads to politics that are reactive, not
proactive.

And it is not just public officials. I have been talking to advocacy groups around the country, working with them and trying to
help them with framing issues. I have worked with more than two
hundred advocacy groups in this way. They have the same problems: They are under attack all the time, and they are trying to
defend themselves against the next attack. Realistically, they do

not have time to plan. They do not have time to think long-term. They do not have time to think beyond their particular issues.

They are all good people, intelligent, committed people. But they are constantly on the defensive. Why? It is not hard to explain it when we think about funding.

The right-wing think tanks get large block grants and endowments. Millions at a time. They are very well funded. The smallest effective think tanks on the right have budgets of four to seven million dollars a year. Those are the *small* operations. The large ones have up to thirty million dollars a year.

Furthermore, they know that they are going to get the money the next year, and the year after that. Remember, these are block grants—no strings attached. Do what you need. Hire intellectuals. Bring talent along. One of the think tanks is putting up a new building. It is going to be an eight-story building with a state-of-the-art media auditorium, and one hundred apartments for interns who cannot afford apartments in Washington.

These institutions also build human capital for the future. The interns and scholars are people who want to be there, who have talents and abilities that may well make them important in their fields. Through the think tanks, they get to know each other. And the interns are building lifetime networks: They are likely to know each other closely throughout their lives because they lived together while they were interns. These are social networks that will pay dividends for years and years. The conservatives who built the think tanks are not dumb people.

There are very few grants like this from progressive foundations. Progressive foundations spread the money around. They give twenty-five thousand dollars here, maybe fifty thousand, maybe even a hundred thousand. Sometimes it is a big grant. But recipients have to do something different from what everyone else is doing because the foundations see duplication as wasting money. Not only that, but they are not block grants; the recipients do not have full freedom to decide how to spend the money. And it is certainly not appropriate to use it for career development or infrastructure building or hiring intellectuals to think about long-term as well as short-term or interrelated policies. The emphasis is on providing direct services to the people who need the services: grassroots funding, not infrastructure creation. This is, for the most part, how progressive foundations work. And because of that, the organizations they fund have to have a very narrow focus. They have to have projects, not just areas they work on. Activists and advocates are overworked and underpaid, and they do not have time or energy to think about how they should be linking up with other people. They mainly do not have the time or training to think about framing their issues. The system forces a narrow focus—and with it, isolation.

You ask, Why is it like this? There is a reason. There is a deep reason, and it is a reason you should all think about. In the right's hierarchy of moral values, the top value is preserving and defending the moral system itself. If that is your main goal, what do you do? You build infrastructure. You buy up media in advance. You plan ahead. You do things like give fellowships to right-wing law students to get them through law school if they join the Federalist Society. And you get them nice jobs after that. If you want to extend your worldview, it is very smart to make sure that over the long haul you have the people and the resources that you need.

On the left, the highest value is helping individuals who need help. So if you are a foundation or you are setting up a foundation, what makes you a good person? You help as many people as you can. And the more public budgets get cut, the more people there are who need help. So you spread the money around to the grassroots organizations, and therefore you do not have any money left for infrastructure or talent development, and certainly not for intellectuals. Do not waste a penny in duplicating efforts, because you have to help more and more people. How do you show that you are a good, moral person or foundation? By listing all the people you help; the more the better.

And so you perpetuate a system that helps the right. In the process, it also does help people. Certainly, it is not that people do not need help. They do. But what has happened as budgets and taxes get cut is that the right is privatizing the left. The right is forcing the left to spend ever more private money on what the government should be supporting.

There are many things that we can do about all this. Let's talk about where to start.

The right knows how to talk about values. We need to talk about values. If we think about it a little, we can list our values. But it is not easy to think about how the values fit the issues, to know how to talk about every issue from the perspective of our values, not theirs. Progressives have a lot to learn from the Rockridge Institute's nonpartisan research on the values—both conservative and progressive—behind the issues.

Progressives also have to look at the integration of issues. This is something that the right is very, very savvy about. They know about what I call *strategic initiatives*. A strategic initiative is a plan in which a change in one carefully chosen issue area has automatic effects over many, many, many other issue areas.

For example, tax cuts. This seems straightforward, but as a result there is not enough money in the budget for *any* of the government's social programs. Not just not enough money for, say, homelessness or schools or environmental protection; instead, not enough money for everything at once, the whole range. This is a strategic initiative.

Or tort reform, which means putting limits on awards in lawsuits. Tort reform is a top priority for conservatives. Why do conservatives care so much about this? Well, as soon as you see the effects, you can see why they care. Because in one stroke you prohibit all of the potential lawsuits that will be the basis of future environmental legislation and regulation. That is, it is not just regulation of the chemical industry or the coal industry or the nuclear power industry or other things that are at stake. It is the regulation of *everything*. If parties who are harmed cannot sue immoral or negligent corporations or professionals for significant sums, the companies are free to harm the public in unlimited ways in the course of making money. And lawyers, who take risks and make significant investments in such cases, will no longer make enough money to support the risk. And corporations will be free to ignore the public good. That is what "tort reform" is about.

In addition, if you look at where Democrats get much of their money in the individual states, it is significantly from the lawyers who win tort cases. Many tort lawyers are important Democratic donors. Tort "reform"—as conservatives call it—cuts off this source of money. All of a sudden three-quarters of the money going to the Texas Democratic Party is not there. In addition, companies who poison the environment want to be able to cap possible awards. That way they can calculate in advance the cost of paying victims and build it into the cost of doing business. Irresponsible corporations win big from tort reform. The Republican Party wins big from tort reform. And these real purposes are hidden. The issue appears to be eliminating "frivolous lawsuits"—people getting thirty million dollars for having hot coffee spilled on them.

However, what the conservatives are really trying to achieve is not in the proposal. What they are trying to achieve *follows* from enacting the proposal. They don't care primarily about the lawsuits themselves. They care about getting rid of environmental, consumer, and worker protections in general. And they care about defunding the Democratic Party. That is what a strategic initiative is.

There have been a couple of strategic initiatives on the left—environmental impact reports and the Endangered Species Act—but it has been thirty years since they were enacted.

Unlike the right, the left does not think strategically. We think issue by issue. We generally do not try to figure out what minimal change we can enact that will have effects across many issues.

There are a very few exceptions. For example, at the present moment there is a strategic proposal called the New Apollo Initiative. Simply put, the idea is to put thirty billion dollars a year—which is the amount that now goes in subsidies to support the coal and gas industries—into alternative energy. What makes this strategic? It is strategic because it is not just an energy issue or a sustainability issue. It is also:

- A jobs issue: It would create two to four million jobs.
- A health issue: Less air pollution means less childhood asthma.
- A clean water, clean air issue.
- A species issue: It would clean up environments and habitats.
- A global warming issue: We would be making a contribution to lowering greenhouse gases without a program specifically for global warming.
- A foreign policy issue: We would no longer be dependent on Middle Eastern oil.
- A third world development issue: Every country, no matter how "underdeveloped," can make its own energy if it has the appropriate alternative technologies. Such countries would not have to borrow money to buy oil and pollute their environments. And they would not have to pay interest on the money borrowed. Furthermore, every dollar invested in energy in the third world has a multiplier effect of six.

In short, a massive investment in alternative energy has an enormous yield over many issue areas. This is not just about energy; it is about jobs, health, clean air and water, habitat, global warming, foreign policy, and third world development. It is also about putting together new coalitions and organizing new institutions and new constituencies.

Thirty billion dollars a year for ten years put into alternative energy would have massive effects. But progressive candidates are still thinking in much smaller terms, not long-term and strategically.

There are also strategic initiatives of another kind—what I call slippery slope initiatives: Take the first step and you're on your way off the cliff. Conservatives are very good at slippery slope initiatives. Take "partial-birth abortion." There are almost no such cases. Why do conservatives care so much? Because it is a first step down a slippery slope to ending all abortion. It puts out there a frame of abortion as a horrendous procedure, when most operations ending pregnancy are nothing like this.

Why an education bill about school testing? Once the testing frame applies not just to students but also to *schools*, then schools can, metaphorically, fail—and be punished for failing by having their allowance cut. Less funding in turn makes it harder for the schools to improve, which leads to a cycle of failure and ultimately elimination for many public schools. What replaces the public school system is a voucher system to support private schools. The wealthy would have good schools—paid for in part by what used to be tax payments for public schools. The poor would not have the money for good schools. We would wind up with a two-tier school system, a good one for the "deserving rich" and a bad one for the "undeserving poor."

The Medicare bill was another slippery slope initiative. The HMOs can use their size to bargain for lower prices on drugs, while the government is forbidden from using its size to get discounts. Moreover, Medicare will be forced to compete with private drug companies after a few years on uneven grounds; the drug companies will get a twelve-billion-dollar subsidy to help attract senior citizens. The conservative strategy is to lure seniors out of Medicare and into private accounts with temporarily lower drug prices. Eventually, more and more people will leave Medicare, until it collapses. From the conservative moral worldview, that is how it should be.

And yet a prominent Democratic senator voted for it, on the grounds that it would give immediate help in billions of dollars to seniors in her home state. She called it a "good first step." To the edge of the cliff.

The conservatives don't have to win on issue after issue after issue. There is a lot you can do about it. Here are eleven things progressives can do.

**First, recognize what conservatives have done right and where progressives have missed the boat.** It is more than just control of the media, though that is far from trivial. What they have done right is to successfully frame the issues from their perspective. Acknowledge their successes and our failures.

**Second, remember "Don't think of an elephant."** If you keep their language and their framing and just argue against it, you lose because you are reinforcing their frame.

**Third, the truth alone will not set you free.** Just speaking truth to power doesn't work. You need to frame the truths effectively from your perspective.

**Fourth, you need to speak from your moral perspective at all times.** Progressive policies follow from progressive values. Get clear on your values and use the language of values. Drop the language of policy wonks.

**Fifth, understand where conservatives are coming from.** Get their strict father morality and its consequences clear. Know what you are arguing against. Be able to explain why they believe what they believe. Try to predict what they will say.

**Sixth, think strategically, across issue areas.** Think in terms of large moral goals, not in terms of programs for their own sake.

**Seventh, think about the consequences of proposals.** Form progressive slippery slope initiatives.

**Eighth, remember that voters vote their identity and their values, which need not coincide with their self-interest.**

**Ninth, unite! And cooperate!** Here's how: Remember the six modes of progressive thought: (1) socioeconomic, (2) identity politics, (3) environmentalist, (4) civil libertarian, (5) spiritual, and (6) antiauthoritarian. Notice which of these modes of thought you use most often—where you fall on the spectrum and where the people you talk to fall on the spectrum. Then rise above your own mode of thought and start thinking and talking from shared progressive values.

**Tenth, be proactive, not reactive. Play offense, not defense.** *Practice reframing, every day, on every issue.* Don't just say what you believe. Use *your* frames, not their frames. Use them because they fit the values you believe in.

**Eleventh, speak to the progressive base in order to activate the nurturant model of "swing voters." Don't move to the right.** Rightward movement hurts in two ways. It alienates the progressive base and it helps conservatives by activating their model in swing voters.

## — 2 —

# Enter the Terminator!

— OCTOBER 13, 2003 —

Newspaper and TV reporters require a story. Each story requires a frame. How was the election of Arnold Schwarzenegger framed? Here is a selection:

**Voter Revolt:** *Gray Davis was such a bad governor that the voters justifiably ousted him and voted in the representative of the other party.*

**The Great Noncommunicator:** *Gray Davis governed as well as possible under the circumstances, but was so bad at communicating with the electorate that he could not communicate his real accomplishments, nor could he communicate the role of the Republicans in the state's problems. The public thought Davis was worse than he was, and wanted a communicator, so they voted him out and chose an actor.*

**Those Kooky Californians:** *People in California are so weird that they voted a politically inexperienced bodybuilder-actor into office to replace a governor they voted for just last year.*

**The People Beat the Politicians:** *When the people win, politics as usual must lose (Schwarzenegger's acceptance speech).*

**Just a Celebrity:** *People don't understand politics and just voted for a celebrity.*

**Up by His Bootstraps:** *Coming here as an immigrant, Arnie worked and worked to become a champion bodybuilder, then a millionaire actor, and finally achieved his dream—becoming governor.*

Framing was rampant in reporting in this election. Frames come with inferences, so each frame implies something different.

The **Voter Revolt** frame legitimizes the recall. It assumes that Davis was incompetent or corrupt; that the voters correctly perceived this; that it outraged them; that they spontaneously, righteously, and overwhelmingly rose up and ousted him, replacing him with someone they knew to be more competent. Democracy was served and all is well. We should be happy about the result and things will be better.

The **Great Noncommunicator** frame implies that the one and only problem was Gray Davis's inability to communicate. It assumes he was a competent governor and a responsible administrator with that single fatal flaw, and that people want communication so badly they recalled Davis because he couldn't communicate his achievements. The implication is that the recall and Schwarzenegger's election had nothing to do with anything outside California or anything broader, and that the problem just was Davis.

The **Kooky Californians** frame says the recall was irrational, that Californians can't tell the movies from reality, that a movie action hero can't govern a great state in trouble, that Arnie is a political incompetent, and that chaos will ensue.

The **People Beat the Politicians** frame is Schwarzenegger's attempt to impose his own frame. The context is that Arnold will have to deal with a majority Democratic legislature. This frame casts him and the Republican politicians as "the people" and the Democrats as "politics as usual," which "the people" voted against.

The **Just a Celebrity** frame implies that there were no partisan politics in this election and that any celebrity at all could just as well have won.

The **Up by His Bootstraps** frame attributes Schwarzenegger's election principally to Arnold himself, especially to his hard work and ambition. Arnold got to be governor because he deserved it. He deserved it because he worked hard—at bodybuilding, acting, and campaigning.

If there's going to be a news story there's going to be a frame, and each frame will have different inferences.

## — Facts and Framing —

It is a general finding about frames that if a strongly held frame doesn't fit the facts, the facts will be ignored and the frame will be kept. The frames listed above don't do very well at fitting the facts—though each has a grain of truth. Let's look at the facts that each frame hides.

The **Voter Revolt** frame hides the national Republican effort over several years to make Davis look bad by hurting the California economy. It hides the fact that energy deregulation was brought in by Republican governor Pete Wilson. It ignores the fact that there was no real energy crisis. It resulted from thievery by Enron and other heavy Bush contributors, thievery that was protected by the Federal Energy Regulatory Commission, run by Bush appointees. The Bush administration looked the other way while California was being bilked and went to great lengths not to help California financially in any of the many ways the federal government can help. Schwarzenegger had had a meeting with Ken Lay and other energy executives in spring 2001 when Lay was promoting deregulation, but denies any complicity in the theft. Schwarzenegger is now promoting energy deregulation again.

It also ignores the fact that California's Republican legislature went out of its way to make Davis look bad, refusing to support reasonable measures for dealing with the budget problems. It ignores the fact that the recall petition was paid for by a wealthy conservative legislator, that signature gatherers were paid handsomely, and that some signatures were from out of state, which is illegal. And it ignores the enormous amount of money and organization put into the Schwarzenegger campaign by Republicans. This was no simple popular revolution. Most of all, the Voter Revolt frame does not explain why Schwarzenegger should have been the candidate chosen.

The **Great Noncommunicator** frame has a lot of truth to it. But it too hides all the sustained Republican effort, and it hides the fact that it is not just Gray Davis, but rather Democrats in general, who cannot communicate effectively.

The **Kooky Californians** frame does not explain any of the above. The Republicans' long-term, carefully structured anti-Davis campaign is hidden by this frame. It is as if there were no politics at work here at all.

The **People Beat the Politicians** frame hides the fact that the Republicans have been playing politics with the state finances for years in an attempt to beat Davis. It hides the fact that the Schwarzenegger team, run by former governor Pete Wilson, will be just as much "politics as usual," and that the Democratic representatives in the legislature numerically represent more of "the people" than do the Republicans.

The **Just a Celebrity** frame ignores all the above political factors, and also cannot explain why *this particular celebrity* won. Jay Leno supported Schwarzenegger. Leno is just as much a celebrity, but he could never have been elected governor.

The **Up by His Bootstraps** frame also ignores all the politics involved and doesn't explain why other movie actors who pulled themselves up by their bootstraps didn't run and wouldn't have been elected.

These framings hide other important facts as well. They don't explain why a lot of union rank-and-file members ignored their unions' support of Davis and voted for Schwarzenegger against their self-interest. They don't explain why a great many Hispanics voted for Schwarzenegger instead of Cruz Bustamante. They don't explain Schwarzenegger's popularity with women, despite the revelations of his sexist behavior.

### The Moral Politics Analysis

I'm going to offer a very different account of the Schwarzenegger victory, based on my book *Moral Politics*. Since the book was written in 1996 and updated in 2002, the account I'll be giving is a general one, based on a general understanding of American politics, not on the special facts about this election. My resulting claim is that much of what occurred in the recall election is the same as what has been going on for some time in American politics. The Schwarzenegger election, I propose, should not be seen as an entirely unique event, despite having unique elements, but rather part of the overall political landscape.

In *Moral Politics*, I suggested that voters vote their identity— they vote on the basis of who they are, what values they have, and who and what they admire. A certain number of voters identify themselves with their self-interest and vote accordingly. But that is the exception rather than the rule. There are other forms of personal identification—with one's ethnicity, with one's values, with cultural stereotypes, and with culture heroes. As far as elections are concerned, the most powerful forms of identification are with values and corresponding cultural stereotypes. The Republicans have discovered this, and it is a major reason why they have been winning elections—despite being in a minority. Democrats have not yet figured this out.

The *Moral Politics* discovery is that models of idealized family structure lie at the heart of our politics—less literally than metaphorically. The very notion of the founding *fathers* uses a metaphor of the nation as family, not as something we think actively about, but as way of structuring our understanding of the enormous hard-to-conceptualize social group, the nation, in terms of something closer to home, the family. It is something we do automatically, usually without consciously thinking about it.

Our politics are organized around two opposite and idealized models of the family: the strict father and nurturant parent models.

The nurturant parent family assumes that the world, despite its dangers and difficulties, is basically good, can be made better, and that it is one's responsibility to work toward that. Accordingly, children are born good and parents can make them better. Both parents share responsibility for raising the children. Their job is to nurture their children and raise their children to be nurturers. Nurturing has two aspects: empathy (feeling and caring how others feel) and responsibility (for taking care of oneself and others for whom we are responsible). These two aspects of nurturance imply family values that we can recognize as progressive political values: from empathy, we want for others protection from harm, fulfillment in life, fairness, freedom (consistent with responsibility), and open two-way communication. From responsibility follow competence, trust, commitment, community building, and so on.

From these values, specific policies follow: governmental protection in the form of a social safety net and government regulation, as well as the military and the police (from protection), universal education (from competence, fairness), civil liberties and equal treatment (from fairness and freedom), accountability (from trust), public service (from responsibility), open government (from open communication), and the promotion of an economy that benefits all (from fairness) and functions to promote these values (from responsibility).

The role of government is to provide the infrastructure and services to enact these values, and taxes are the dues you pay to live in such a civilized society. In foreign policy the role of the nation should be to promote cooperation and extend these values to the world. These are traditional progressive values in American politics.

The conservative worldview is shaped by very different family values.

The strict father model assumes that the world is and always will be dangerous and difficult, and that children are born bad and must be made good. The strict father is the moral authority who has to support and defend the family, tell his wife what to do, and teach his kids right from wrong. The only way to do that is through painful punishment—physical discipline that by adulthood will develop into internal discipline. Morality and survival jointly arise from such discipline—discipline to follow moral precepts and discipline to pursue your self-interest to become self-reliant. The good people are the disciplined people. Once grown, the self-reliant, disciplined children are on their own, and the father is not to meddle in their lives. Those children who remain dependent (who were spoiled, overly willful, or recalcitrant) should be forced to undergo further discipline or should be cut free with no support to face the discipline of the outside world.

Project this onto the nation and you have the radical right-wing politics that has been misnamed "conservative." The good citizens are the disciplined ones—those who have already become wealthy or at least self-reliant—and those who are on the way. Social programs "spoil" people, giving them things they haven't earned and keeping them dependent. They are therefore evil and to be eliminated. Government is there only to protect the nation, maintain order, administer justice (punishment), and to provide for the orderly conduct of and the promotion of business. Business (the market) is the mechanism by which the disciplined people become self-reliant, and wealth is a measure of discipline. Taxes beyond the minimum needed for such government are punishments that take away from the good, disciplined people rewards that they have earned, and spend it on those who have not earned it.

In foreign affairs the government should maintain its sovereignty and impose its moral authority everywhere it can, while seeking its self-interest (the economic self-interest of corporations and military strength).

### How We Vote
Given these distinctions, there are the natural complications of real people. Such models are there in the synapses of our brains. When we vote on the basis of values and cultural stereotypes, what determines how we vote is which model is active for understanding politics at the time.

We all have *both* models—either actively or passively. Progressives who can understand an Arnold Schwarzenegger movie have at least a passive version of the strict father model alongside the active nurturant model that defines their politics. Conservatives who can understand *The Cosby Show* have at least a passive version of the nurturant model.

But many people—often enough to decide elections—have active versions of *both* models that they use in different parts of their lives. There are strict fathers in the classroom who have progressive politics. There are strict fathers on the job who are nurturant parents at home. Many blue-collar workers are strict fathers at home, but nurturant toward their coworkers. Union employees tend to be strict toward their employers and nurturant toward union members. Women tend to have active nurturant parent models, but a significant number accept the authority of the strict father, are strict mothers, or may have some significant fear. Fear triggers the strict father model; it tends to make the model active in one's brain.

What conservatives have learned about winning elections is that they have to activate the strict father model in more than half the electorate—either by fear or by other means. The September 11 attacks gave the Bush administration a perfect mechanism for winning elections: They declared an unending war on terror. The frame of the "War on Terror" presupposes that the populace should be terrified, and orange alerts and other administration measures and rhetoric keep the terror frame active. Fear and uncertainty then naturally activate the strict father frame in a majority of people, leading the electorate to see politics in conservative terms.

### Enter the Terminator

Enter the Terminator: the ultimate in strictness, the tough guy extraordinaire. The world champion bodybuilder is the last word in discipline. What better stereotype for strict father morality? That is the reason that it was Schwarzenegger—not just any celebrity like Jay Leno or Rob Lowe or Barbra Streisand—who could activate a strict stereotype and with it conservative Republican values.

What is peculiar to California is Arnold and the culture of the movies. But the same mechanism lay behind the Republican victories in the 2002 election and in elections around the country since the days of Ronald Reagan, but especially in the last decade, when Republicans mastered the art form of activating the strict father image in the minds of voters. Schwarzenegger's popularity with Californians has the same source as Bush's popularity with the NASCAR dads: identification with strict father values and stereotypes. Moreover, Davis's inability to communicate strong progressive values is hardly unique to him. Democrats nationwide have a similar inability to effectively and strongly communicate their values and evoke powerful progressive stereotypes.

In addition, Davis made the bad mistake of accepting the Democratic Leadership Council's metaphor of campaigning as marketing. In the DLC model, you look for a list of particular issues that a majority of people, including those on the left, support. In the last congressional election it was prescription drugs, social security, and a woman's right to choose. If necessary, you "move to the right"—adopt some right-wing values in hope of getting "centrist" voters. Davis, for example, favored the death penalty and tough sentencing, and supported the prison guards' union. It's a self-defeating strategy. Conservatives have been winning elections without moving to the left.

By presenting a laundry list of issues, Davis and other Democrats fail to present a moral vision—a coherent identity with a powerful cultural stereotype—that defines the very identity of the voters they are trying to reach. A list of issues is not a moral vision. Indeed, many Democrats were livid that Schwarzenegger did not run on the issues. He didn't need to. His very being activated the strict father model—the heart of the moral vision of conservative Republicans, and the most common response to fear and uncertainty.

In short, Schwarzenegger's victory is right in line with other conservative Republican victories. Davis's defeat is right in line with other Democratic defeats. Unless the Democrats realize this, they will not learn the lesson of this election.

### Right-Wing Power Grabs

Indeed, conservatives are busy trying to keep Democrats from learning this lesson. There is an important frame we haven't mentioned yet: the Right-Wing Power Grab frame. Davis used this at the beginning of his campaign, and Clinton and the Democratic presidential candidates who supported Davis echoed the frame. This frame does accurately characterize many of the facts as we have discussed them. But Davis was unable to communicate this frame effectively, and it fell from public sight. The day after the election it was one of the few frames *not* mentioned by the mainstream media. It has been dropped by the Democrats but kept alive by the Republicans, who are using it to taunt and delegitimize Democrats. They are using the Voter Revolt frame to argue that the Right-Wing Power Grab frame was inaccurate.

Here's how the argument goes: The Right-Wing Power Grab frame implicitly accuses the Schwarzenegger campaign of deception, of failing to admit connections to Karl Rove and the national Republican apparatus, and of misrepresenting the facts—many of which have been discussed previously. A "power grab" is illegitimate, using either illegal or immoral means to attain power. Using some of the frames we have discussed, the Republicans manipulated the media to hide facts and create false impressions. From the perspective of the facts presented previously, the election does seem to fit the Right-Wing Power Grab frame.

In the wake of the election the Republicans have grabbed on to the Democrats' previous use of the Right-Wing Power Grab frame, arguing from the Voter Revolt interpretation of the election to claim that there was no power grab at all, that the election simply expressed the will of the voters. The very fact that Schwarzenegger got a strong plurality—and near majority—in the election is used as prima facie evidence that the Voter Revolt frame is the correct way to interpret the election. But as we have seen, that frame hides the facts that the Right-Wing Power Grab frame illuminates.

The Democrats ignore the power of framing at their peril.

# 3

# What's in a Word? Plenty, if It's *Marriage*

— FEBRUARY 18, 2004 —

What's in a word? Plenty, if the word is *marriage*.

Marriage is central to our culture. Marriage legally confers many hundreds of benefits, but that is only its material aspect. Marriage is an institution, the public expression of lifelong commitment based on love. It is the culmination of a period of seeking a mate, and, for many, the realization of a major goal, often with a build-up of dreams, dates, gossip, anxiety, engagement, a shower, wedding plans, rituals, invitations, a bridal gown, bridesmaids, families coming together, vows, and a honeymoon. Marriage is the beginning of family life, commonly with the expectation of children and grandchildren, family gatherings, in-laws, Little League games, graduations, and all the rest.

Marriage is also understood in terms of dozens of deep and abiding metaphors: a journey through life together, a partnership, a union, a bond, a single object of complementary parts, a haven, a means for growth, a sacrament, a home. Marriage confers a social status—a married couple with new social roles. And for a great many people, marriage legitimizes sex. In short, marriage is a big deal.

In arguing against same-sex marriage, the conservatives are using two powerful ideas: definition and sanctity. We must take them back. We have to fight definition with definition and sanctity with sanctity. As anthropological studies of American marriage have shown, they got the definition wrong. Marriage, as an ideal, is defined as "the realization of love through a lifelong public commitment." Love is sacred in America. So is commitment. There *is* sanctity in marriage: It is the sanctity of love and commitment.

Like most important concepts, marriage also comes with a

variety of prototypical cases: The ideal marriage is happy, lasting, prosperous, and with children, a nice home, and friendships with other married couples. The typical marriage has its ups and downs, its joys and difficulties, typical problems with children and in-laws. The nightmare marriage ends in divorce, due perhaps to incompatibility, abuse, or betrayal. It is a rich concept.

None of the richness we have just discussed requires marriage to be heterosexual—not its definition, its sanctity, its rituals, its family life, its hopes and dreams. The locus of the idea that mar-riage is heterosexual is in a widespread cultural stereotype.

In evoking this stereotype, language is important. The radical right uses *gay marriage*. Polls show most Americans overwhelm-ingly against antigay discrimination, but equally against "gay mar-riage." One reason, I believe, is that *marriage* evokes the idea of sex, and most Americans do not favor gay sex. Another is that the stereotype of marriage is heterosexual. *Gay* for the right connotes a wild, deviant, sexually irresponsible lifestyle. That's why the right prefers *gay marriage* to *same-sex marriage*.

But *gay marriage* is a double-edged sword. President Bush chose not to use the words *gay marriage* in his State of the Union address. I suspect that the omission occurred for a good reason. His posi-tion is that *marriage* is defined as being between a man and a woman, and so the term *gay marriage* should be an oxymoron, as meaningless as *gay apple* or *gay telephone*. The more *gay marriage* is used, the more normal the idea of same-sex marriage becomes, and the clearer it becomes that *marriage* is not defined to exclude the very possibility. This is exactly why some gay activists want to use *same-sex marriage* or even *gay marriage*.

Because marriage is central to family life, it has a political dimen-sion. As I discuss in my book *Moral Politics*, conservative and pro-gressive politics are organized around two very different models of married life: a strict father family and a nurturing parent family.

The strict father is moral authority and master of the house-hold, dominating the mother and children and imposing needed discipline. Contemporary conservative politics turns these family values into political values: hierarchical authority, individual discipline, military might. Marriage in the strict father family must be heterosexual marriage: The father is manly, strong, decisive, dominating—a role model for sons, and for daughters a model of a man to look up to.

The nurturant parent model has two equal parents, whose job is to nurture their children and teach their children to nurture others. Nurturance has two dimensions: empathy and responsibility, for oneself and others. Responsibility requires strength and competence. The strong nurturing parent is protective and caring, builds trust and connection, promotes family happiness and fulfillment, fairness, freedom, openness, cooperation, community development. These are the values of strong progressive politics. Though the stereotype is again heterosexual, there is nothing in the nurturing family model to rule out same-sex marriage.

In a society divided down the middle by these two family models and their politics, we can see why the issue of same-sex marriage is so volatile. What is at stake is more than the material benefits of marriage and the use of the word. At stake are one's identity and most central values. This is not just about same-sex couples. It is about which values will dominate in our society.

When conservatives speak of the "defense of marriage," liberals are baffled. After all, no individual's marriage is being threatened. It's just that more marriages are being allowed. But conservatives see the strict father family, and with it their political values, as under attack. They are right. This is a serious matter for their politics and moral values as a whole. Even civil unions are threatening, since they create families that cannot be traditional strict father families.

Progressives are of two minds. Pragmatic liberals see the issue as one of benefits—inheritance, health care, adoption, and so forth. If that's all that is involved, civil unions should be sufficient—and they certainly are an advance. Civil unions would provide equal material protection under the law. Why not leave civil unions to the state and marriage to the churches, as in Vermont?

Idealistic progressives see beyond the material benefits, important as they are. Most gay activists want more than civil unions. They want full-blown marriage, with all its cultural meanings—a public commitment based on love, all the metaphors, all the rituals, joys, heartaches, family experiences—and a sense of normality, on par with all other people. The issue is one of personal freedom: The state should not dictate who should marry whom. It is also a matter of fairness and human dignity. Equality under the law includes social and cultural as well as material benefits. The slogan here is "freedom to marry."

The Democratic presidential nominees have tried to sidestep the issue. John Kerry and Howard Dean claim marriage is a matter for the church, while the proper role for the state is civil unions and a guarantee of material benefits. This argument makes little sense to me. The ability of ministers, priests, and rabbis to perform marriage ceremonies is granted by governments, not by religions. And civil marriage is normal and widespread. Besides, it will only satisfy the pragmatic liberals. Idealistic conservatives will see civil unions as tantamount to marriage, and idealistic progressives will see them as falling far short of equal protection. It may work in Vermont, but it remains to be seen whether such an attempt to get around the issue will play in most of the country.

And what of the Constitutional amendment to legally define marriage as ocurring between a man and a woman? Conservatives will be for it, and many others with a heterosexual stereotype of marriage may support it. But it's unlikely to get enough progressive support to pass. The real question is, Will the very proposal of such an amendment help George Bush keep the White House?

It's hard to tell right now.

But the progressives who are not running for office can do a lot. Progressives need to reclaim the moral high ground—of the grand American tradition of freedom, fairness, human dignity, and full equality under the law. If they are pragmatic liberals, they can talk this way about the civil unions and material benefits. If they are idealistic progressives, they can use the same language to talk about the social, cultural, and material benefits of marriage. Either way, our job as ordinary citizens is to reframe the debate, in everything we say and write, in terms of our moral principles.

Sanctity is a higher value than economic fairness. Talking about benefits is beside the point when the sanctity of marriage is in dispute. Talk sanctity first. With love and commitment, you have the very definition of the marital ideal—of what marriage is fundamentally about.

We all have to put our ideas out there so that candidates can readily refer to them. For example, when there is a discussion in your office, church, or other group, there is a simple response for someone who says, "I don't think gays should be able to marry. Do you?" The response is: "I believe in equal rights, period. I don't think the state should be in the business of telling people who they can or can't marry. Marriage is about love and commitment, and denying lovers the right to marry is a violation of human dignity."

The media does not have to accept the right wing's frames. What can a reporter ask besides "Do you support gay marriage?" Try this: "Do you think the government should tell people who they can and can't marry?" Or "Do you think the freedom to marry who you want to is a matter of equal rights under the law?" Or "Do you see marriage as the realization of love in a lifetime commitment?" Or "Does it benefit society when two people who are in love want to make a public lifetime commitment to each other?"

Reframing is everybody's job. Especially reporters'.

It has long been right-wing strategy to repeat over and over phrases that evoke their frames and define issues their way. Such repetition makes their language normal, everyday language and their frames normal, everyday ways to think about issues. Reporters have an obligation to notice when they are being taken for a ride and they should refuse to go along. It is a duty of reporters *not* to accept this situation and simply use those right-wing frames that have come to seem natural. And it is the *special duty* of reporters to study framing and to learn to see through politically motivated frames, even if they have come to be accepted as everyday and commonplace.

# 4

# Metaphors of Terror

— September 16, 2001 (edited August 2004) —

## — Our Brains Had to Change —

Everything we know is physically instantiated in the neural systems of our brains.

What we knew before September 11 about America, Manhattan, the World Trade Center, air travel, and the Pentagon were intimately tied up with our identities and with a vast amount of what we took for granted about everyday life. It was all there physically in our neural synapses. Manhattan: the gateway to America for generations of immigrants—the chance to live free of war, pogroms, religious and political oppression!

The Manhattan skyline had meaning in my life, even more than I knew. When I thought of it, I thought of my mother. Born in Poland, she arrived as an infant, grew up in Manhattan; worked in factories for twenty-five years; and had family, friends, a life, a child. She didn't die in concentration camps. She didn't fear for her life. For her America was not all that she might have wanted it to be, but it was plenty.

I grew up in Bayonne, New Jersey, across the bay from that skyline. The World Trade Center wasn't there then, but over the years, as the major feature of the skyline, it became for me, as for others, the symbol of New York—not only the business center of America, but also the cultural center and the communications center. As such, it became a symbol for America itself, a symbol for what it meant to be able to go about your everyday life free of oppression, and just able to live and do your job, whether as a secretary or an artist, a manager or a fireman, a salesman or a teacher or a TV star. I wasn't consciously aware of it, but those images were intimately tied to my identity, both as an individual and as an American. And all that and so much more were there physically as part of my brain on the morning of September 11.

The devastation that hit those towers that morning hit me. Buildings are metaphorically people. We see features—eyes, nose, and mouth—in their windows. I now realize that the image of the plane going into South Tower was for me an image of a bullet going through someone's head, the flames pouring from the other side like blood spurting out. It was an assassination. The tower falling was a body falling. The bodies falling were me, relatives, friends. Strangers who had smiled as they had passed me on the street screamed as they fell past me. The image afterward was hell: ashes, smoke and steam rising, the building skeleton, darkness, suffering, death.

The people who attacked the towers got into my brain, even three thousand miles away. All those symbols were connected to more of my identity than I could have realized. To make sense of this, my very brain had to change. And change it did, painfully. Day and night. By day the consequences flooded my mind; by night the images had me breathing heavily, nightmares keeping me awake. Those symbols lived in the emotional centers of my brain. As their meanings changed, I felt emotional pain.

It was not just me. It was everyone in this country, and many in other countries. The assassins managed not only to kill thousands of people, but also to reach in and change the brains of people all over America.

It is remarkable to know that two hundred million of my countrymen feel as wrenched as I do.

## — The Power of the Images —

As a metaphor analyst, I want to begin with the power of the images and where that power comes from.

There are a number of metaphors for buildings. A common visual metaphor is that buildings are heads, with windows as eyes. The metaphor is dormant, there in our brains, waiting to be awakened. The image of the plane going into South Tower of the World Trade Center activated it. The tower became a head, with windows as eyes, the edge of the tower the temple. The plane going through it became a bullet going through someone's head, the flames pouring from the other side the blood spurting out.

Metaphorically, tall buildings are people standing erect. As each tower fell, it became a body falling. We are not consciously aware of the metaphorical images, but they are part of the power and the horror we experience when we see them.

Each of us, in the premotor cortex of our brains, has what are called mirror neurons. Such neurons fire either when we perform an action or when we see the same action performed by someone else. There are connections from that part of the brain to the emotional centers. Such neural circuits are believed to be the basis of empathy.

This works literally—when we see a plane coming toward the building and imagine people in the building, we feel the plane coming toward us; when we see the building toppling toward others, we feel the building toppling toward us. It also works metaphorically: If we see the plane going through the building, and unconsciously we evoke the metaphor of the building as a head with the plane going through its temple, then *we* sense—unconsciously but powerfully—being shot through the temple. If we evoke the metaphor of the building as a person and see the building fall to the ground in pieces, then we sense—again unconsciously but powerfully—that *we* are falling to the ground in pieces. Our systems of metaphorical thought, interacting with our mirror neuron systems, turn external literal horrors into felt metaphorical horrors.

Here are some other cases:

- **Control is up:** You have control over the situation; you're on top of things. This has always been an important basis of towers as symbols of power. In this case, the toppling of the towers meant loss of control, loss of power.

- **Phallic imagery:** Towers are symbols of phallic power, and their collapse reinforces the idea of loss of power. Another kind of phallic imagery was more central here: the planes penetrating the towers with a plume of heat, and the Pentagon, a vaginal image from the air, penetrated by the plane as missile. These phallic interpretations came from women who felt violated both by the attack and the images on TV.

- **A society is a building:** A society can have a "foundation," which may or may not be solid, and it can "crumble" and "fall." The World Trade Center was symbolic of society. When it crumbled and fell, the threat was to more than a building.

- **Standing:** We think metaphorically of things that perpetuate over time as "standing." During the Gulf War, George H.W. Bush kept saying, "This will not stand," meaning that the situation would not be perpetuated over time. The World Trade Center was built to last ten thousand years. When it crumbled, it metaphorically raised the question of whether American power and American society would last.

- **Building as temple:** Here we had the destruction of the temple of capitalist commerce, which lies at the heart of our society.

- **Our minds play tricks on us:** The image of the Manhattan skyline is now unbalanced. We are used to seeing it with the towers there. Our mind imposes our old image of the towers, and the sight of them gone gives one the illusion of imbalance, as if Manhattan were sinking. Given the symbolism of Manhattan as the promise of America, it appears metaphorically as if that promise were sinking.

- **Hell:** Then there is the persistent image, day after day, of the charred and smoking remains: hell.

The World Trade Center was a potent symbol, tied into our understanding of our country and ourselves in myriad ways. All of what we know is physically embodied in our brains. To incorporate the new knowledge requires a physical change in the synapses of our brains, a physical reshaping of our neural system.

The physical violence was not only in New York and Washington. Physical changes—violent ones—have been made to the brains of all Americans.

## — How the Administration Frames the Event —

The administration's framings and reframings and its search for metaphors should be noted. The initial framing was as a crime with victims, and perpetrators to be "brought to justice" and "punished." The crime frame entails law, courts, lawyers, trials, sentencing, appeals, and so on. It was hours before *crime* changed to *war*, with *casualties, enemies, military action, war powers,* and so on.

Donald Rumsfeld and other administration officials have pointed out that this situation does not fit our understanding of a war. There are enemies and casualties all right, but no enemy army, no regiments, no tanks, no ships, no air force, no battlefields, no strategic targets, and no clear victory. The war frame just doesn't fit. Colin Powell had always argued that no troops should be committed without specific objectives, a clear and achievable definition of victory, and a clear exit strategy, and open-ended commitments should not be used. But he has pointed out that none of these is present in this "war."

Because the concept of war doesn't fit, there is a frantic search for metaphors. First, Bush called the terrorists cowards—but this didn't seem to work too well for martyrs who willingly sacrificed their lives for their moral and religious ideals. More recently he has spoken of "smoking them out of their holes," as if they are rodents, and Rumsfeld has spoken of "drying up the swamp they live in," as if they are snakes or lowly swamp creatures. The conceptual metaphors here are moral is up, immoral is down (they are lowly), and immoral people are animals (that live close to the ground).

The use of the word *evil* in the administration's discourse works in the following way. In conservative, strict father morality (see *Moral Politics*, chapter 5), evil is a palpable thing, a force in the world. To stand up to evil you have to be morally strong. If you're weak you let evil triumph, so that weakness in itself is a form of evil, as is promoting weakness. Evil is inherent, an essential trait, that determines how you will act in the world. Evil people do evil things. No further explanation is necessary. There can be no social causes of evil, no religious rationale for evil, no reasons or arguments for evil. The enemy of evil is good. If our enemy is evil, we are inherently good. Good is our essential nature, and what we do in the battle against evil is good. Good and evil are locked in a battle, which is conceptualized metaphorically as a physical fight in which the stronger wins. Only superior strength can defeat evil, and only a show of strength can keep evil at bay. Not to show overwhelming strength is immoral, since it will induce evildoers to perform more evil deeds, because they'll think they can get away with it. To oppose a show of superior strength is therefore immoral. Nothing is more important in the battle of good against evil, and if some innocent noncombatants get in the way and get hurt, it is a shame, but it is to be expected and nothing can be done about it. Indeed, performing lesser evils in the name of good is justified—"lesser evils" like curtailing individual liberties, sanctioning political assassinations, overthrowing governments, torturing, hiring criminals, and creating "collateral damage."

Then there is the basic security metaphor, security as containment—keeping the evildoers out. Secure our borders, keep them and their weapons out of our airports, have marshals on the planes. Most security experts say that there is no sure way to keep terrorists out or to deny them the use of some weapon or other; a determined, well-financed terrorist organization can penetrate any security system. Or they can choose other targets, say, oil tankers.

Yet the security as containment metaphor is powerful. It is what lies behind the missile shield proposal. Rationality might say that the September 11 attacks showed the missile shield is pointless. But it strengthened the use of the security as containment metaphor. As soon as you say *national security*, the security as containment metaphor will be activated, and with it the missile shield.

## — The Conservative Advantage —

The reaction of the Bush administration is just what you would expect a conservative reaction would be: pure strict father morality. There is evil loose in the world. We must show our strength and wipe it out. Retribution and vengeance are called for. If there are casualties or collateral damage, so be it.

The reaction from liberals and progressives has been far different: *Justice is called for, not vengeance.* Understanding and restraint are what is needed. The model for our actions should be the rescue workers and doctors—the healers—not the bombers.

We should not be like them. We should not take innocent lives in bringing the perpetrators to justice. Massive bombing of Afghanistan—with the killing of innocents—will show that we are no better than they.

But it has been the administration's conservative message that has dominated the media. The event has been framed in their terms. As Newt Gingrich put it on the Fox network, "Retribution *is* justice."

We must reframe the discussion. I have been reminded of Gandhi's words: "Be the change you want." The words apply to governments as well as to individuals.

## — Causes —

There are (at least) three kinds of causes of radical Islamic terrorism:

- Worldview: the religious rationale
- Social and political conditions: cultures of despair
- Means: the enabling conditions

The Bush administration has discussed only the third: the means that enable attacks to be carried out. These include leadership (for example, bin Laden), host countries, training facilities and bases, financial backing, cell organization, information networks, and so on. These do not include the first and second on the list.

### Worldview: The Religious Rationale

The question that keeps being asked in the media is, Why do they hate us so much?

It is important at the outset to separate moderate-to-liberal Islam from radical Islamic fundamentalists, who do not represent most Muslims.

Radical Islamic fundamentalists hate our culture. They have a worldview that is incompatible with the way that Americans—and other Westerners—live their lives.

One part of this worldview concerns women, who are to hide their bodies, should have no right to property, and so on. Western sexuality, mores, music, and women's equality all violate their values, and the ubiquity of American cultural products, like movies and music, throughout the world offends them.

A second part concerns theocracy: They believe that governments should be run by clerics according to strict Islamic law.

A third concerns holy sites, like those in Jerusalem, which they believe should be under Islamic political and military control.

A fourth concerns the commercial and military incursions by Westerners on Islamic soil, which they liken to the invasion of the hated crusaders. The way they see it, our culture spits in the face of theirs.

A fifth concerns jihad—a holy war to protect and defend the faith.

A sixth is the idea of a martyr, a man willing to sacrifice himself for the cause. His reward is eternal glory—an eternity in heaven surrounded by willing young virgins. In some cases there is a promise that his family will be taken care of by the community.

### Social and Political Conditions: Cultures of Despair

Most Islamic would-be martyrs not only share these beliefs but have also grown up in a culture of despair; they have nothing to lose. Eliminate such poverty and you eliminate the breeding ground for most terrorists—though the September 11 terrorists were relatively well-to-do. When the Bush administration speaks of eliminating terror, it does not appear to be talking about eliminating cultures of despair and the social conditions that lead one to want to give up his life to martyrdom.

Princeton Lyman of the Aspen Institute has made an important proposal—that the worldwide antiterrorist coalition being formed should also address the causal real-world conditions. Country by country, the conditions (both material and political) leading to despair need to be addressed, with a worldwide commitment to ending them. It should be done because it is a necessary part of addressing the causes of terrorism—and because it is right! The coalition being formed should be made into a long-term global institution for this purpose.

What about the first cause—the radical Islamic worldview itself? Military action won't change it. Social action won't change it. Worldviews live in the minds of people. How can one change those minds—and if not present minds, then future minds? *The West* cannot! Those minds can only be changed by moderate and liberal Muslims—clerics, teachers, elders, respected community members. There is no shortage of them. I doubt that they are well organized, but the world needs them to be well organized and effective. It is vital that moderate and liberal Muslims form a unified voice against hate and, with it, terror. Remember that *Taliban* means "student." Those who teach hate in Islamic schools must be replaced—and we in the West cannot replace them. This can only be done by an organized moderate, nonviolent Islam. The West can make the suggestion and offer extensive resources, but we alone are powerless to carry it out. We depend on the goodwill and courage of moderate Islamic leaders. To gain it, we must show our goodwill by beginning in a serious way to address the social and political conditions that lead to despair.

But a conservative government, thinking of the enemy as evil, will not take the primary causes seriously. They will only go after the enabling causes. But unless the primary causes are addressed, terrorists will continue to be spawned.

### — Public Discourse —

The Honorable Barbara Lee (D-Calif.), who I am proud to acknowledge as my representative in Congress, in casting the lone vote against giving President Bush full Congressional approval for carrying out his War on Terrorism as he sees fit, said the following:

> I am convinced that military action will not prevent further acts of international terrorism against the United States. This is a very complex and complicated matter.
>
> . . . However difficult this vote may be, some of us must urge the use of restraint. Our country is in a state of mourning. Some of us must say, let us step back for a moment. Let us just pause for a minute and think through the implications of our actions today so that this does not spiral out of control.

> I have agonized over this vote, but I came to grips
> with it today and I came to grips with opposing this
> resolution during the very painful yet very beautiful
> memorial service. As a member of the clergy so elo-
> quently said, "As we act, let us not become the evil
> that we deplore."

I agree. But what is striking to me as a linguist is the use of neg-
atives in the statement: "not prevent," "restraint" (inherently negative), "not spiral out of control," "not become the evil that we
deplore." Friends are circulating a petition calling for "justice
*without* vengeance." *Without* has another implicit negative. It is
not that these negative statements are wrong. But what is needed
is a *positive* form of discourse.

There is one.

The central concept is that of responsibility, which is at the heart
of progressive/liberal morality. (See *Moral Politics*.) Progressive/lib-
eral morality begins with *empathy*, the ability to understand others
and feel what they feel. That is presupposed in *responsibility*—responsibility for oneself, for protection, for the care of those who need
care, and for the community. Those were the values that we saw in
action among the rescue workers in New York right after the attack.

Responsibility requires competence and effectiveness. If you are
to deal responsibly with terrorism, you must deal effectively with *all*
its causes: religious, social, and enabling. The enabling causes must
be dealt with effectively. Bombing innocent civilians and harming
them by destroying their country's domestic infrastructure will be
counterproductive—as well as immoral. Responsibility requires
*care* in the place of blundering, overwhelming force.

Massive bombing would be irresponsible. Failure to address the
religious and social causes would be irresponsible. The responsible
response begins with joint international action to address *all three*:
the social and political conditions *and* the religious worldview *and*
the means, with all due care.

— Foreign Policy —

At a time when terrorist threats come from groups of *individuals* rather than states, when wars occur *within nations*, when "free markets" exist *without freedom*, when *overpopulation* threatens stability, when *intolerant cultures* limit freedom and promote violence, when *transnational corporations* act like oppressive governments, and when the *oil economy* threatens the planet's future, the central problems in today's world cannot be solved by state-level approaches.

The state-level part of the answer is to recognize global interdependence and focus foreign policy on diplomacy, alliances, international institutions and strong defensive and peacekeeping forces, with war as a last resort.

But what is needed even more is a new kind of moral foreign policy, one that realizes that America can only be a better America if the world is a better world. America must become a moral leader using fundamental human values: caring and responsibility carried out with strength to respond to the world's problems.

In a values-based foreign policy, issues that were not previously seen as part of foreign policy become central. Women's education is the best way to alleviate overpopulation and promote development. Renewable energy could make the world oil-independent. Food, water, health, ecology, and corporate reform are foreign policy issues, as are rights: rights of women, children, workers, prisoners, refugees, and political minorities.

These issues have been left to international advocacy groups, and many are doing excellent work. But these issues need an integrated approach that requires a foreign policy that is serious about addressing them.

Why have these issues been largely defined as outside the foreign policy arena?

The metaphors that foreign-policy experts have used to define what foreign policy *is* rule out these important concerns. The metaphors involve self-interest (for example, the rational actor model), stability (a physics metaphor), industrialization (unindustrialized nations are "underdeveloped"), and trade (freedom is free trade).

There is an alternative way of thinking about foreign policy under which all these issues would become a natural part of what foreign policy is about. The premise is that when international relations work smoothly, it is because certain moral norms of the international community are being followed. This mostly goes unnoticed, since those norms are usually followed. We notice problems when those norms are breached. Given this, it makes sense that foreign policy should be centered around those norms.

The moral norms I suggest come out of what in *Moral Politics* I called nurturant morality. It is a view of ethical behavior that centers on empathy and responsibility (for yourself and others needing your help). Many things follow from these central principles: fairness, minimal violence (for example, justice without vengeance), an ethic of care, protection of those needing it, a recognition of interdependence, cooperation for the common good, the building of community, mutual respect, and so on. When applied to foreign policy, nurturant moral norms would lead the American government to uphold the Anti-Ballistic Missile (ABM) Treaty, sign the Kyoto accords, engage in a form of globalization governed by an ethics of care—and it would automatically make all the concerns listed above (such as the environment and women's rights) part of our foreign policy.

This, of course, implies (1) multilateralism, (2) interdependence, and (3) international cooperation. But these three principles, without nurturant norms, could equally well apply to a radically conservative foreign policy. Bush's foreign policy, as he announced in the 2000 election campaign, has been one of self-interest ("what's in the best interest of the United States")—if not outright hegemony (the Cheney/Rumsfeld position). The Democratic leaders have incorrectly criticized Bush for being isolationist and unilateralist on issues like the Kyoto accords and the

ABM Treaty. He was neither isolationist nor unilateralist. He was just following his stated policy of self-interest, using strict father morality as his guide.

Imagine if Bush had happened to receive the full support of France, Germany, and the UN when he announced his policy. Then he would have been called an internationalist and multilateralist. When it is in America's interest (as he sees it), he will work with those nations willing to go along, "the coalition of the willing." Whether Bush looks like a multilateralist depends on who is willing. Self-interest crosses the boundaries between unilateralism and multilateralism. The Bush foreign policy is one of unyielding self-interest.

There is, interestingly, an apparent overlap between the nurturant norms policy and an idealistic vision of the Bush administration's new war. The overlap is, simply, that it is a moral norm to refuse to engage in or support terrorism. From this perspective, it looks like left and right are united. It is an illusion.

In nurturant norms policy, antiterrorism arises from another moral norm: *Violence against innocent parties is immoral.* But Bush's new war will certainly not follow *that* moral norm. Bush's military advisers appear to be planning massive bombings and infrastructure destruction that will certainly take the lives of a great many innocent civilians.

Within a year of the end of the Gulf War, the CIA reported that about a million Iraqi civilians had died from the effects of the war and the embargo—many from disease and malnutrition due to the U.S. destruction of water treatment plants, hospitals, electric generation plants, and so on, together with the inability to get food and medical supplies. Many more innocents have since died from the effects of the war. Do we really think that the United States will have the protection of innocent Afghans in mind if it rains terror down on the Afghan infrastructure? We are supposedly fighting *them* because they immorally killed innocent civilians. That made them evil. If *we* do the same, are we any less immoral?

This argument would hold water if the Bush "War on Terrorism" were really about morality in the way that morality is understood by progressives/liberals. It is not. In conservative morality, there is a fight between good and evil, in which "lesser evils" are tolerated and even seen as necessary and expected.

The argument that killing innocent civilians in retaliation would make us as bad as them works for liberals, not for conservatives.

The idealistic claim of the Bush administration is they intend to wipe out all terrorism. What is not mentioned is that the United States has systematically promoted a terrorism of its own and has trained terrorists, from the contras to the mujahideen, the Honduran death squads, and the Indonesian military. Will the U.S. government stop training terrorists? Of course not. It will deny that it does so. Is this duplicity? Not in terms of conservative morality and its view of good versus evil and "lesser evils."

If the administration's discourse offends us, we have a moral obligation to change public discourse!

*Be the change you want!* If the United States wants terror to end, the United States must end its own contribution to terror. And we must also end terror sponsored not against the West but against others. We have made a deal with Pakistan to help in Afghanistan. Is it part of the deal that Pakistan renounce its own terrorism in Kashmir against India? I would be shocked if it were. The Bush foreign policy of self-interest does not require it.

The question must be asked. If that is not part of the deal, then our government has violated its own stated ideals; it is hypocritical. If the terrorism we don't mind—or might even like—is perpetuated, terrorism will not end and will eventually turn back on us, just as our support for the mujahideen did.

We must be the change we want!

The foreign policy of moral norms is the only sane foreign policy. In the idea of responsibility for oneself, it remains practical. But through empathy and other forms of responsibility (protection, care, competence, effectiveness, community development), it would lead to international cooperation and a recognition of interdependence.

## — Domestic Policy —

I have a rational fear, a fear that the September 11 attack has given the Bush administration a free hand in pursuing a conservative domestic agenda. This has so far been unsayable in the media. But it must be said, lest it happen for sure.

Where are the forty billion dollars coming from? Not from a rise in taxes. The sacrifices will not be made by the rich. Where, then? The only available source I can think of is the Social Security "lockbox," which is now wide open. The conservatives have been trying to raid the Social Security fund for some time, and the Democrats had fought them off until now. A week ago, the suggestion to take forty billion dollars from the Social Security "surplus" would have been indefensible. Has it now been done—with every Democratic senator voting for it, and all but one of the Democrats in Congress?

Think of it: Your retirement contributions—and mine—are going to fight Bush's "war." No one dares to talk about it that way. It's just forty billion dollars, as if it came out of nowhere. No one says that forty billion dollars come from your retirement contributions. No one talks about increasing taxes. We should at least ask just where the money is coming form.

If the money is coming from Social Security, then Bush has achieved a major goal of his partisan conservative agenda— without fanfare, without notice, and with the support of virtually all Democrats.

Calling for war instead of mere justice has given the conservatives free rein. I fear it will only be a matter of time before they claim that we need to drill for oil in the Alaskan Wildlife Refuge for national security reasons. If that most pristine place falls, they will use the national security excuse to drill and mine coal all over the country. The energy program will be pushed through as a matter of national security. All social programs will be dismissed for lack of funds, which will be diverted to national security.

Dick Cheney has said that this war may never be completed. Newt Gingrich estimates at least four or five years, certainly past the 2004 election. With no definition of victory and no exit strategy, we may be entering a state of *perpetual war.* This would be very convenient for the conservative domestic agenda: The war machine will determine the domestic agenda, which will allow conservatives to do whatever they want domestically in the name of national security.

The recession we are entering has already been blamed on The Attack, not on Bush's economic policies. Expect a major retrenchment on civil liberties. Expect any WTO protesters to be called terrorists and/or traitors. Expect any serious opposition to Bush's policies to be called traitorous.

Who has the courage to frankly discuss domestic policy at this time?

*Since this was written, a* New York Times *editorial acknowledged that the money is coming from the Social Security "lockbox." A Wall Street Journal editorial called for the president to take advantage of the moment to push his overall agenda through. Senator Frank Murkowski introduced a rider on the war appropriations bill, authorizing drilling in the Arctic National Wildlife Preserve. And the forty billion dollars has become two hundred billion.*

# — 5 —

# Metaphors That Kill

— MARCH 18, 2003 —

*Metaphors can kill.*

That's how I began a piece on the Gulf War back in 1990, just before the war began. (See http://philosophy.uoregon.edu/metaphor/lakoff-l.htm.) Many of those metaphorical ideas are back, but within a very different and more dangerous context. Since the Iraq War is due to start any day, perhaps even tomorrow, it might be useful to take a look before the action begins at the metaphorical ideas being used to justify the Iraq War.

One of the central metaphors in our foreign policy is that a nation is a person. It is used hundreds of times a day, every time the nation of Iraq is conceptualized in terms of a single person, Saddam Hussein. The war, we are told, is not being waged against the Iraqi people, but only against this one person. Ordinary American citizens are using this metaphor when they say things like "Saddam is a tyrant. He must be stopped." What the metaphor hides, of course, is that the three thousand bombs to be dropped in the first two days will not be dropped on that one person. They will kill many thousands of people hidden by the metaphor, people that we are, according to the metaphor, *not* going to war against.

The nation as a person metaphor is pervasive, powerful, and part of an elaborate metaphor system. It is part of an international community metaphor, in which there are friendly nations, hostile nations, rogue states, and so on. This metaphor comes with a notion of the national interest: Just as it is in the interest of a person to be healthy and strong, so it is in the interest of a nation-person to be economically healthy and militarily strong. That is what is meant by the "national interest."

In the international community, peopled by nation-persons, there are nation-adults and nation-children, with maturity metaphorically understood as industrialization. The children are the "developing" nations of the third world, in the process of industrializing, who need to be taught how to develop properly and must be disciplined (say, by the International Monetary Fund) when they fail to follow instructions. "Backward" nations are those that are "underdeveloped." Iraq, despite being the cradle of civilization, is seen via this metaphor as a kind of defiant, armed teenage hoodlum who refuses to abide by the rules and must be taught a lesson.

The international relations community adds to the nation as a person metaphor what is called the rational actor model. The idea here is that it is irrational to act against your interests, and that nations act as if they were rational actors—individual people trying to maximize their gains and assets and minimize their costs and losses. In the Gulf War, the metaphor was applied so that a country's "assets" included its soldiers, materiel, and money. Since the United States lost few of those "assets" in the Gulf War, the war was reported, just afterward in the *New York Times* business section, as having been a "bargain." Because Iraqi civilians were not our assets they could not be counted among the "losses," and so there was no careful public accounting of civilian lives lost, people maimed, and children starved or made seriously ill by the war or the sanctions that followed it. Estimates vary from half a million to a million or more. However, public relations was seen to be a U.S. asset: Excessive slaughter reported in the press would be bad PR, a possible loss. These metaphors are with us again. A short war with few U.S. casualties would be minimize costs. But the longer it goes on, the more Iraqi resistance and the more U.S. casualties, the less the United States would appear invulnerable and the more the war would appear as a war against the Iraqi people. That would be a high "cost."

According to the rational actor model, countries act naturally in their own best interests—preserving their assets, that is, their own populations, their infrastructures, their wealth, their weaponry, and so on. That is what the United States did in the Gulf War and what it is doing now. But Saddam Hussein, in the Gulf War, did not fit our government's rational actor model. He had goals like preserving his power in Iraq and being an Arab hero just for standing up to the Great Satan. Though such goals might have their own rationality, they are "irrational" from the model's perspective.

One of the most frequent uses of the nation as a person metaphor comes in the almost daily attempts to justify the war metaphorically as a "just war." The basic idea of a just war uses the nation as a person metaphor, plus two narratives that have the structure of classical fairy tales: the self-defense story and the rescue story.

In each story there is a hero, a crime, a victim, and a villain. In the self-defense story the hero and the victim are the same. In both stories the villain is inherently evil and irrational: The hero can't reason with the villain; he has to fight him and defeat or kill him. In both, the victim must be innocent and beyond reproach. In both, there is an initial crime by the villain, and the hero balances the moral books by defeating him. If all the parties are nation-persons, then self-defense and rescue stories become forms of a just war for the hero-nation.

In the Gulf War, George H. W. Bush tried out a self-defense story: Saddam was "threatening our oil lifeline." The American people didn't buy it. Then he found a winning story, a rescue story: the "rape" of Kuwait. It sold well, and is still the most popular account of that war.

In the Iraq War, George W. Bush is pushing different versions of the same two story types, and this explains a great deal of what is going on in the American press and in speeches by Bush and Powell. If they can show that Saddam Hussein equals Al-Qaeda— that he is helping or harboring Al-Qaeda—then they can make a case for the self-defense scenario, and hence for a just war. Or if weapons of mass destruction ready to be deployed are found, the self-defense scenario can be justified in another way. Indeed, despite the lack of any positive evidence and the fact that the secular Saddam and the fundamentalist bin Laden despise each other, the Bush administration has managed to convince 40 percent of the American public of the link just by asserting it. The administration has told its soldiers the same thing, and so our military personnel see themselves as going to Iraq in defense of their country. In the rescue scenario the victims are (1) the Iraqi people and (2) Saddam's neighbors, whom he has not attacked but is seen as threatening. That is why Bush and Powell keep on listing Saddam's crimes against the Iraqi people and the weapons he could use to harm his neighbors. Again, most of the American people have accepted the idea that the Iraq War is a rescue of the Iraqi people and a safeguarding of neighboring countries. Actually, the war threatens the safety and well-being of the Iraqi people.

And why such enmity toward France and Germany? Via the nation as a person metaphor, they are supposed to be our "friends," and friends are supposed to be supportive and jump in and help us when we need help. Friends are supposed to be loyal. That makes France and Germany fair-weather friends! Not there when you need them.

This is how the war is being framed for the American people by the administration and the media. Millions of people around the world can see that the metaphors and fairy tales don't fit the current situation, that the Iraq War does not qualify as a just war—a "legal" war. But if you accept all these metaphors, as Americans have been led to do by the administration, the press, and the lack of an effective Democratic opposition, then the Iraq War would indeed seem like a just war.

But surely most Americans have been exposed to the facts—the lack of a credible link between Saddam and Al-Qaeda, no WMDs found, and the idea that large numbers of innocent Iraqi civilians will be killed or maimed by our bombs. Why don't they reach the rational conclusion?

One of the fundamental findings of cognitive science is that people think in terms of frames and metaphors—conceptual structures like those we have been describing. The frames are in the synapses of our brains, physically present in the form of neural circuitry. When the facts don't fit the frames, the frames are kept and the facts ignored.

It is a common folk theory of progressives that "the facts will set you free." If only you can get all the facts out there in the public eye, then every rational person will reach the right conclusion. It is a vain hope. Human brains just don't work that way. Framing matters. Frames once entrenched are hard to dispel.

In the Gulf War, Colin Powell began the testimony before Congress. He explained the rational actor model to Congress and gave a brief exposition of the views on war of Clausewitz, the Prussian general: War is business and politics are carried out by other means. Nations naturally seek their self-interest, and when necessary they use military force in the service of their self-interest. This is both natural and legitimate.

To the Bush administration, this war furthers our self-interest in controlling the flow of oil from the world's second-largest known reserve, and in being in the position to control the flow of oil from central Asia. This would guarantee energy domination over a significant part of the world. The United States could control oil sales around the world. And in the absence of alternative fuel development, whoever controls the worldwide distribution of oil controls politics and economics.

My 1990 paper did not stop the Gulf War. This paper will not stop the Iraq War. So why bother?

I think it is crucially important to understand the cognitive dimensions of politics—especially when most of our conceptual framing is unconscious and we may not be aware of our own metaphorical thought. I have been referred to as a "cognitive activist," and I think the label fits me well. As a professor I do analyses of linguistic and conceptual issues in politics, and I do them as accurately as I can. But that analytic act is a political act. Awareness matters. Being able to articulate what is going on can change what is going on—at least in the long run.

This war is a symptom of a larger disease. The war will start presently. The fighting will be over before long. Where will the antiwar movement be then?

- First, the antiwar movement, properly understood, is not just, or even primarily, a movement against the war. It is a movement against the overall direction that the Bush administration is moving in.
- Second, to be effective such a movement needs to say clearly what it is for, not just what it is against.
- Third, it must have a clearly articulated moral vision, with values rather than mere interests determining its political direction.

As the war begins, we should look ahead to transforming the antiwar movement into a movement that powerfully articulates progressive values and moves our nation toward achieving those values. The war has begun a discussion about values. Let's continue it.

# 6

## Betrayal of Trust: Beyond Lying

— SEPTEMBER 15, 2003 —

The question of the L-word keeps coming up. Did the president and his chief advisors *lie?* I think this is the wrong question to be asking. The real issue is betrayal of trust.

The president has been criticized for using the following as justifications for the Iraq War. We went to war in Iraq because Saddam Hussein had weapons of mass destruction that threatened us. He was reconstituting his nuclear weapons programs (the aluminum tubes, the uranium from Africa). He had huge stocks of chemical and biological weapons that could be launched quickly in aerial vehicles and that threatened the United States. Saddam was working with Al-Qaeda. Iraqis had "trained Al-Qaeda members in bomb making and poisons and deadly gases."

It appears these were all falsehoods. The tubes couldn't be used for enriching uranium, there was no uranium anyway, and no reconstituted nuclear weapons programs. The vast stockpiles of chemical and biological weapons have not been found, and by now would be well past their use date. The aerial-delivery vehicles could not go more that a few hundred miles and could not threaten the United States. There is no evidence that Saddam had anything to do with the Al-Qaeda attack on the United States, or that there was any cooperation between Saddam and Al-Qaeda, although 70 percent of Americans believe it, according to a recent *Washington Post* poll, and perhaps a higher percentage of men and women in the military.

President Bush's speech on September 7, 2003, used language that had the same implications. "[We] acted first in Afghanistan, by destroying training camps of terror, and removing the regime that harbored Al-Qaeda. . . . And we acted in Iraq, where the former regime sponsored terror, possessed and used weapons of mass destruction. . . . Two years ago, I told the Congress and the country that the war on terror would be a lengthy war, a different kind of war, fought on many fronts in many places. Iraq is now the central front."

Here is the impression that a great many Americans have been left with, especially our men and women in the military and their families: We went to war in Iraq, first to defend our country against terrorists, second to liberate that country—selflessly, at great sacrifice, not out of self-interest.

These are false impressions, and the president continues to create and reinforce them.

Are they *lies*, or are they merely *exaggerations*, *misleading statements*, *mistakes*, *rhetorical excesses*, and so on? Linguists study such matters. The most startling finding is that in considering whether a statement is a lie, the *least* important consideration for most people is whether it is true!

The more important considerations are, *Did he believe it? Did he intend to deceive? Was he trying to gain some advantage or to harm someone else? Is it a serious matter or a trivial one? Is it just a matter of political rhetoric?* Most people will grant that even if the statement happened to be false, if he believed it, wasn't trying to deceive, and was not trying to gain advantage or harm any one, then there was no lie. If it was a lie in the service of a good cause, then it was a white lie. If it was based on faulty information, then it was an honest mistake. If it was just there for emphasis, then it was an exaggeration.

These have been among the administration's defenses. The good cause: liberating Iraq. The faulty information: from the CIA. The emphasis: enthusiasm for a great cause. Even though there is evidence that the president and his advisers knew the information was false, they can deflect the use of the L-word. The falsehoods have been revealed and they, in themselves, do not matter much to most people.

But lying in itself is not and should not be the issue. The real issue is a betrayal of trust. Our democratic institutions require trust. When the president asks Congress to consent to war—the most difficult moral judgment it can make—Congress must be able to trust the information provided by the administration. When the president asks our fighting men and women to put their lives on the line for a reason, they must be able to trust that the reason he has given is true. It is a betrayal of trust for the president to ask our soldiers to risk their lives under false pretenses. And when the president asks the American people to put their sons and daughters in harm's way and to spend money that could be used for schools, for health care, for helping desperate people, for rebuilding decaying infrastructure, and for economic stimulation in hard times, it is a betrayal of trust for the president to give false impressions.

What was *not* in the president's September 7 speech is telling. He sought help from other nations, but he refused to relinquish control over the shaping of Iraq's military, political, and economic future. To a large extent it was the issue of such control that prompted the UN Security Council's refusal to participate in the American attack and occupation. The reason for the resentment against the United States, both in Europe and elsewhere, stemmed from a widespread perception that American interests really lay behind the invasion of Iraq. Those interests are control over the Iraqi economy by American corporations, the political shaping of Iraq to suit U.S. economic and strategic interests, military bases to enhance U.S. power in the Middle East, the elimination of an important enemy of Israel, reconstruction profits to U.S. corporations, control over the future of the second-largest oil supply in the world, and refining and marketing profits for U.S. and British oil companies. The Iraqi people would get profits only from the sale of crude oil, and those profits would substantially go to pay American companies like Halliburton for reconstruction.

In other words, it looks like the war was for long-term U.S.

control of the Middle East and for the self-interest of American corporations, and not a selfless war of liberation. We see this in the administration's arguments that since the United States has shed the blood of its soldiers and spent billions, it is entitled to such spoils of war. This is not an argument from selflessness. It is an investment argument: The war was an expensive investment, and the United States deserves the return on the investment of lives and money. Such arguments make the war look like much more like a self-interested enterprise than mere self-defense and a selfless war of liberation.

If the real rationale for the Iraq War has been self-interested control—over oil resources, the regional economy, political influence, and military bases—if it was not self-defense and not selfless liberation, then President Bush *betrayed the trust* of our soldiers, the Congress, and the American people. Mere lying is a minor matter when betrayal is the issue.

# PART TWO

# FROM THEORY TO ACTION

# 7

## What the Right Wants

There are a number of basic variations on right-wing ideology. Each of them is a version of strict father morality. Some versions are defined by a given domain. Strict father morality applied to the domains of religion, business, and everyday social life characterizes religious, financial, and social conservatives. A focus on unimpeded pursuit of self-interest—and with it, extreme limits on state power over the individual—defines the libertarian strain of right-wing thought. And neocons? As far as I have been able to discern, neocons believe in the unbridled use of power (including state power) to extend the reign of strict father values and ideas into every domain, domestic and international. Neocons are very much concerned with ideas, and tend to have an intellectual strain. They sometimes run up against libertarians, who object to the use of governmental power. Finally, there are warrior conservatives, who identify themselves as warriors on every front in the culture war against liberals and progressives.

On the whole the right wing is attempting to impose a strict father ideology on America and, ultimately, the rest of the world. Although the details vary somewhat with the type of conservative, there are general tendencies. Many progressives underestimate just how radical an ideology this is. Here is an account of what the radical right seems to have in mind.

**God.** Many conservatives start with a view of God that makes conservative ideology seem both natural and good. God is all good and all powerful, at the top of a natural hierarchy in which morality is linked with power. God wants good people to be in charge. Virtue is to be rewarded—with power. God therefore wants a hierarchical society in which there are moral authorities who should be obeyed.

God makes laws—commandments—defining right and wrong. One must have discipline to follow God's commandments. God is punitive: He punishes those who do not follow his commandments, and rewards those who do. Following God's laws takes discipline. Those who are disciplined enough to be moral are disciplined enough to become prosperous and powerful.

God is the original strict father.

Christ, as savior, gives sinners a second chance—a chance to be born again and be obedient to God's commandments this time around.

**The moral order.** Traditional power relations are taken as defining a natural moral order: God above man, man above nature, adults above children, Western culture above non-Western culture, America above other nations. The moral order is all too often extended to men above women, whites above non-whites, Christians above non-Christians, straights above gays.

**Morality.** Preserving and extending the conservative moral system (strict father morality) is the highest priority.

Morality comes in the form of rules, or commandments, made by a moral authority. To be moral is to be obedient to that authority. It requires internal discipline to control one's natural desires and instead follow a moral authority.

Discipline is learned in childhood primarily through punishment for wrongdoing. Morality can be maintained only through a system of rewards and punishments.

**Economics.** Competition for scarce resources also imposes discipline, and hence serves morality. The discipline required to be moral is the same discipline required to win competitions and prosper.

The wealthy people tend to be the good people, a natural elite. The poor remain poor because they lack the discipline needed to prosper. The poor, therefore, deserve to be poor and serve the wealthy. The wealthy need and deserve poor people to serve them. The vast and increasing gap between rich and poor is thus seen to be both natural and good.

To the extent that markets are "free," they are a mechanism for the disciplined (stereotypically good) people to use their discipline to accumulate wealth. Free markets are moral: If everyone pursues his own profit, the profit of all will be maximized. Competition is good; it produces optimal use of resources and disciplined people, and hence serves morality. Regulation is bad; it gets in the way of the free pursuit of profit. Wealthy people serve society by investing and giving jobs to poorer people. Such a division of wealth ultimately serves the public good, which is to reward the disciplined and let the undisciplined be forced to learn discipline or struggle.

**Government.** Social programs are immoral. By giving people things they haven't earned, social programs remove the incentive to be disciplined, which is necessary for both morality and prosperity. Social programs should be eliminated. Anything that could be done by the private sphere should be. Government does have certain proper roles: to protect the lives and the private property of Americans, to making profit seeking as easy as possible for worthy Americans (the disciplined ones), and to promote conservative morality (strict father morality) and religion.

**Education.** Since preserving and extending conservative morality is the highest goal, education should serve that goal. Schools should teach conservative values. Conservatives should gain control of school boards to guarantee this. Teachers should be strict, not nurturant, in the example they set for students and in the content they teach. Education should therefore promote discipline, and undisciplined students should face punishment. Unruly students should face physical punishment (for instance, paddling), and intellectually undisciplined students should not be coddled, but should be shamed and punished by not being promoted. Uniform testing should test the level of discipline. There are right and wrong answers, and they should be tested for. Testing defines fairness: Those who pass are rewarded; those not disciplined enough to pass are punished.

Because immoral, undisciplined children can lead moral, disciplined children astray, parents should be able to choose to which schools they send their children. Government funding should be taken from public schools and given to parents in the form of vouchers. This will help wealthier (more disciplined and moral) citizens send their children to private or religious schools that teach conservative values and impose appropriate discipline. The vouchers given to poorer (less disciplined and less worthy) people will not be sufficient to allow them to get their children into the better private and religious schools. Schools will thus come to reflect the natural divisions of wealth in society. Of course, students who show exceptional discipline and talent should be given scholarships to the better schools. This will help maintain the social elite as a natural elite.

**Health care.** It is the responsibility of parents to take care of their children. To the extent that they cannot, they are not living up to their individual responsibility. No one has the responsibility of doing other people's jobs for them. Thus prenatal care, postnatal care, health care for children, and care for the aged and infirm are matters of individual responsibility. They are not the responsibility of taxpayers.

**Same-sex marriage and abortion.** Same-sex marriage does not fit the strict father model of the family; it goes squarely against it. A lesbian marriage has no father. A gay marriage has "fathers" who are taken to be less than real men. Since preserving and extending the strict father model is the highest moral value for conservatives, same-sex marriage constitutes an attack on the conservative value system as a whole, and on those whose very identity depends on their having strict father values.

Abortion works similarly. There are two stereotypical cases where women need abortions: unmarried teenagers who have been having "illicit" sex, and older women who want to delay child rearing to pursue a career. Both of these fly in the face of the strict father model. Pregnant teenagers have violated the commandments of the strict father. Career women challenge the power and authority of the strict father. Both should be punished by bearing the child; neither should be able to avoid the consequences of their actions, which would violate the strict father model's idea that morality depends on punishment. Since conservative values in general are versions of strict father values, abortion stands as a threat to conservative values and to one's identity as a conservative.

Conservatives who are "pro-life" are mostly, as we have seen, against prenatal care, postnatal care, and health care for children, all of which have major causal effects on the life of a child. Thus they are not really pro-life in any broad sense. Conservatives for the most part are using the idea of terminating a pregnancy as part of a cultural-war strategy to gain and maintain political power.

Both same-sex marriage and abortion are stand-ins for the general strict father values that define for millions of people their identities as conservatives. That is the reason why these are such hot-button issues for conservatives.

To understand this is not to ignore the real pain and difficulty involved in decisions made by individual women to terminate a pregnancy. For those truly concerned with the lives and health of children, the decision to end a pregnancy for whatever reason is always painful and anything but simple. It is this pain that conservatives are exploiting when they use ending pregnancy as a wedge issue in the cultural civil war they have been promoting.

There are also those who are genuinely pro-life, who believe that life begins with conception, that life is the ultimate value, and who therefore support prenatal care, postnatal care, health insurance for poor children, and early childhood education, and who oppose the death penalty, war, and so on. They also recognize that any woman choosing to end a pregnancy is making a painful decision, and empathize with such women and treat them without a negative judgment. These are pro-life progressives—often liberal Catholics. They are not conservatives who use the question of ending pregnancy as a political wedge to gain support for a broader moral and political agenda.

**Nature.** God has given man dominion over nature. Nature is a resource for prosperity. It is there to be used for human profit.

**Corporations.** Corporations exist to provide people with goods and services, and to make profits for investors. They work most efficiently when they seek to maximize their profits. When corporations profit, society profits.

**Regulation.** Government regulation stands in the way of free enterprise, and should be minimized.

**Rights.** Rights must be consistent with morality. Strict father morality defines the limits of what is to count as a "right."

Thus there is no right to an abortion, no right to same-sex marriage, no right to health care (or any other government assistance), no right to know how the administration decides policy, no right to a living wage, and so on.

**Democracy.** A strict father democracy is an institutional democracy operating under strict father values. It counts as a democracy in that it has elections, a tripartite government, civilian control of the military, free markets, basic civil liberties, and widely accessible media. But strict father values are seen as central to democracy—to the empowerment of individuals to change their lives and their society by pursuing their individual interests.

**Foreign Policy.** America is the world's moral authority. It is a superpower because it deserves to be. Its values—the right values—are defined by strict father morality. If there is to be a moral order in the world, American sovereignty, wealth, power, and hegemony must be maintained and American values—conservative family values, the free market, privatization, elimination of social programs, domination of man over nature, and so on—spread throughout the world.

**The Culture War.** Strict father morality defines what a good society is. The good society is threatened by liberal and progressive ideas and programs. That threat must be fought at all costs. The very fabric of society is at stake.

Those are the basics. Those are the ideas and values that the right wing wants to establish, nothing less than a radical revolution in how America and the rest of the world functions. The vehemence of the culture war provoked and maintained by conservatives is no accident. For strict father morality to gain and maintain political power, disunity is required. First, there is economic disunity, the two-tier economy with the "unworthy" poor remaining poor and serving the "deserving" rich. But to stay in power the conservatives need the support of many of the poor. That is, they need a significant percentage of the poor and middle class to vote against their economic interests.

This has been achieved through the recognition that many working people and evangelical Protestants have a strict father morality in their families and/or religious lives. Conservative intellectuals have realized that these are the same values that drive political conservatism. They have also realized that people vote their values and their identities more than their economic self-interests. What they have done is to create, via framing and language, a link between strict father morality in the family and religion on the one hand and conservative politics on the other. This conceptual link must be so emotionally strong that it can overcome economic self-interest.

Their method for achieving this has been the cultural civil war— a civil war carried out with everything short of live ammunition— pitting Americans with strict father morality (called conservatives) against Americans with nurturant parent morality (the hated liberals), who are portrayed as threatening the way of life and the cultural, religious, and personal identities of conservatives.

Conservative political and intellectual leaders faced a challenge in carrying out their goals. They represented an economic and political elite, but they were seeking the votes of middle- and lower-class working people. They needed, therefore, to identify conservative ideas as populist and liberal/progressive ideas as elitist—even though the reverse was true. They faced a massive framing problem, a problem that required a change in everyday language and thought. But strict father morality gave them an important advantage: It suggests that the wealthy have earned their wealth, that they are good people who deserve it.

Through the work of their think tank intellectuals, their language professionals, their writers and ad agencies, and their media specialists, conservatives have worked a revolution in thought and language over thirty to forty years. Through language they have branded liberals (whose policies are populist) as effete elitist, unpatriotic spendthrifts—limousine liberals, latte liberals, tax-and-spend liberals, Hollywood liberals, East Coast liberals, the liberal elite, wishy-washy liberals, and so on. At the same time they have branded conservatives (whose policies favor the economic elite) as populists—again through language, including body language. From Ronald Reagan's down-home folksiness to George W. Bush's John Wayne–style "Bubbaisms," the language, dialects, body language, and narrative forms have been those of rural populists. Their radio talk show hosts—warriors all—have adopted the style of hellfire preachers. But the message is the same: The hated liberals, who are effete, elitist, unpatriotic spendthrifts, are threatening American culture and values, and have to be fought vigorously and continuously on every front. It is a threat to the very security of the nation, as well as morality, religion, the family, and everything real Americans hold dear. Their positions on wedge issues—guns, babies, taxes, same-sex marriage, the flag, school prayer—reveal the "treachery" of liberals. The wedge issues are not important in themselves, but are vital in what they represent: a strict father attitude to the world.

Without the cultural civil war, the conservatives cannot win.

# 8

## What Unites Progressives

To approach what unites progressives, we must first ask what divides them. Here are some of the common parameters that divide progressives from one another:

- Local interests
- Idealism versus pragmatism
- Radical change versus moderate change
- Militant versus moderate advocacy
- Types of thought processes: socioeconomic, identity politics, environmentalist, civil libertarian, spiritual, and antiauthoritarian (see *Moral Politics* for details)

Programs are a major problem for attempts at unity. As soon as a program is made specific, the differences must be addressed. Progressives tend to talk about programs. But programs are not what most Americans want to know about. Most Americans want to know what you stand for, whether your values are their values, what your principles are, what direction you want to take the country in. In public discourse, values trump programs, principles trump programs, policy directions trump programs. I believe that values, principles, and policy directions are exactly the things that can unite progressives, if they are crafted properly. The reason that they can unite us is that they stand conceptually above all the things that divide us.

### — Ideas that Make Us Progressives —

What follows is a detailed explication of each of those unifying ideas:

- First, *values* coming out of a basic progressive vision
- Second, *principles* that realize progressive values
- Third, *policy directions* that fit the values and principles
- And fourth, a *brief ten-word philosophy* that encapsulates all the above

### The Basic Progressive Vision

The basic progressive vision is of community—of America as family, a caring, responsible family. We envision an America where people care about each other, not just themselves, and act responsibly with strength and effectiveness for each other.

We are all in the same boat. Red states and blue states, progressives and conservatives, Republicans and Democrats. United, as we were for a brief moment just after September 11, not divided by a despicable culture war.

### The Logic of Progressive Values

The progressive core values are family values—those of the responsible, caring family.

**Caring and responsibility, carried out with strength.** These core values imply the full range of progressive values. Here are those progressive values, together with the logic that links them to the core values.

**Protection, fulfillment in life, fairness.** When you *care about* someone, you want them to *be protected from harm*, you want their *dreams to come true*, and you want them to be *treated fairly*.

**Freedom, opportunity, prosperity.** There is no *fulfillment* without *freedom*, no *freedom* without *opportunity*, and no *opportunity* without *prosperity*.

**Community, service, cooperation.** Children are shaped by their *communities*. Responsibility requires *serving* and helping to shape your community. That requires *cooperation*.

**Trust, honesty, open communication.** There is no *cooperation* without *trust*, no *trust* without *honesty*, and no *cooperation* without *open communication*.

Just as these values follow from caring and responsibility, so every other progressive value follows from these. Equality follows from fairness, empathy is part of caring, diversity is from empathy and equality.

Progressives not only share these values, but also share political principles that arise from these values.

### Progressive Principles

**Equity.** What citizens and the nation owe each other. If you work hard; play by the rules; and serve your family, community, and nation, then the nation should provide a decent standard of living, as well as freedom, security, and opportunity.

**Equality.** Do everything possible to guarantee political equality and avoid imbalances of political power.

**Democracy.** Maximize citizen participation; minimize concentrations of political, corporate, and media power. Maximize journalistic standards. Establish publicly financed elections. Invest in public education. Bring corporations under stakeholder control, not just stockholder control.

**Government for a better future.** Government does what America's future requires and what the private sector cannot do—or is not doing—effectively, ethically, or at all. It is the job of government to promote and, if possible, provide sufficient protection, greater democracy, more freedom, a better environment, broader prosperity, better health, greater fulfillment in life, less violence, and the building and maintaining of public infrastructure.

**Ethical business.** Our values apply to business. In the course of making money by providing products and services, businesses should not adversely affect the public good, as defined by the above values.

**Values-based foreign policy.** The same values governing domestic policy should apply to foreign policy whenever possible.

Here are a few examples where progressive domestic policy translates into foreign policy:

- Protection translates into an effective military for defense and peacekeeping.
- Building and maintaining a strong community translates into building and maintaining strong alliances and engaging in effective diplomacy.
- Caring and responsibility translate into caring about and acting responsibly for the world's people; world health, hunger, poverty, and ecology; population control (and the best method, women's education); and rights for women, children, prisoners, refugees, and ethnic minorities.

All of these would be concerns of a values-based foreign policy.

### Policy Directions

Given progressive values and principles, progressives can agree on basic policy directions. Policy directions are at a higher level than specific policies. Progressives divide on specific policy details while agreeing on directions. Here are some of the many policy directions they agree on.

**The economy.** An economy centered on innovation that creates millions of good-paying jobs and provides every American a fair opportunity to prosper.

**Security**. Through military strength, strong diplomatic alliances, and wise foreign and domestic policy, every American will be safeguarded at home, and America's role in the world will be strengthened by helping people around the world live better lives.

**Health.** Every American should have access to a state-of-the-art, affordable health care system.

**Education.** A vibrant, well-funded, and expanding public education system, with the highest standards for every child and school, where teachers nurture children's minds and often the children themselves, and where children are taught the truth about their nation—its wonders and its blemishes.

**Early childhood.** Every child's brain is shaped crucially by early experiences. We support high-quality early childhood education.

**Environment.** A clean, healthy, and safe environment for ourselves and our children: water you can drink and air you can breathe. Polluters pay for the damage they cause.

**Nature.** The natural wonders of our country are to be preserved for future generations.

**Energy.** We need to make a major investment in renewable energy, for the sake of millions of jobs that pay well, independence from Middle Eastern oil, improvements in public health, preservation of our environment, and the effort to halt global warming.

**Openness.** An open, efficient, and fair government that tells the truth to our citizens and earns the trust of every American.

**Equal rights.** We support equal rights in every area involving race, ethnicity, gender, and sexual orientation.

**Protections.** We support keeping and extending protections for consumers, workers, retirees, and investors.

These and many other policy directions follow from our values and our principles.

### Ten-Word Philosophies

The conservatives have figured out their own values, principles, and directions, and have gotten them out in the public mind so effectively over the past thirty years that they can evoke them all in a ten-word philosophy: Strong Defense, Free Markets, Lower Taxes, Smaller Government, Family Values. We progressives have a different ten-word philosophy, but it won't be as meaningful yet because it will take us a while to get our values, principles, and directions out there. My nomination for our ten-word philosophy versus theirs is the following:

| PROGRESSIVES | CONSERVATIVES |
|---|---|
| Stronger America | Strong Defense |
| Broad Prosperity | Free Markets |
| Better Future | Lower Taxes |
| Effective Government | Smaller Government |
| Mutual Responsibility | Family Values |

A **stronger America** is not just about defense, but about every dimension of strength: our effectiveness in the world, our economy, our educational system, our health care system, our families, our communities, our environment, and so forth.

**Broad prosperity** is the effect that markets are supposed to bring about. But all markets are constructed for someone's benefit; no markets are completely free. Markets should be constructed for the broadest possible prosperity, and they haven't been.

Americans want and deserve a **better future**—economically, educationally, environmentally, and in all other areas of life—for themselves and their children. Lowering taxes, primarily for the super-rich elite, has had the effect of defunding programs that would make a better future possible in all these areas. The proper goal is a better future for all Americans.

Smaller government is, in conservative propaganda, supposed to eliminate waste. It is really about eliminating social programs. **Effective government** is what we need our government to accomplish to create a better future.

Conservative family values are those of a strict father family—authoritarian, hierarchical, every man for himself, based around discipline and punishment. Progressives live by the best values of both families and communities: **mutual responsibility**, which is authoritative, equal, two-way, and based around caring, responsibility (both individual and social), and strength.

The remarkable thing is just how much progressives do agree on. These are just the things that voters tend to care about most: our values, our principles, and the direction in which we want to take the nation.

I believe that progressive values *are* traditional American values, that progressive principles are fundamental American principles, and that progressive policy directions point the way to where most Americans really want our country to go. The job of unifying progressives is really the job of bringing our country together around its finest traditional values.

# 9

# FAQ

Any brief discussion of framing and moral politics will leave many questions unanswered. Here are the most common questions I've gotten.

**There is an asymmetry between *strict father* and *nurturant parent*. Why is the first masculine and the second gender-neutral?**
In the strict father model, the masculine and feminine roles are very different, and the father is the central figure. The strict father is the moral authority of the family, the person in charge of the family, while mothers are seen as being "mommies"—they may be loving, but they are unable to protect and support the family and aren't strict enough to punish their children when they do wrong. Think of the expression "Wait till Daddy gets home," which refers to a strict daddy.

In this strict father model, "mommies" are supposed to uphold the authority of the strict father, but they are not able to do the job themselves. In the nurturant parent model, there just isn't a gender distinction of this sort. Both parents are there to nurture their children, and to raise them to be nurturers. That doesn't mean there won't be gender-based divisions of labor around the house in real life, but they are not within the nurturant parent model.

These models are, of course, stereotypes—idealized, incomplete, oversimplified mental models. Mental models of this sort necessarily differ from real world cases: strict mothers, single-parent households, gay parents, and so on.

**Conservative commentators like David Brooks have referred to the Republicans as the "daddy party" and the Democrats as the "mommy party." Would you agree?**
Here Brooks and others have acknowledged the nation as family

metaphor, and have acknowledged that the strict father model is behind conservative Republican politics. However, such a characterization of the "mommy party" is based on "mommy" in their own conservative, strict father model. What they mean by "mommy party" is that although Democrats may care and be loving people, they just aren't tough and realistic enough to do the job.

This is, of course, completely inaccurate from the Democrats' own liberal/progressive perspective. In a nurturant family, both parents are not just caring but also responsible and strong enough to carry out those responsibilities. This is far from *mommy* in the way the conservatives scornfully use the term. Democrats have been able to successfully provide both protection for and prosperity to the nation.

Conservatives seem not to understand what nurturant morality is about, both in the family and the nation. They find any view that is not strict to be "permissive." Nurturant parenting is, of course, anything but permissive, with its stress on teaching children to be responsible for themselves and empathetic and responsible toward others, and raising them to be strong and well-educated enough to carry out their responsibilities. The conservatives parody liberals as permissive, as supporting a feel-good morality—doing whatever feels good. The conservatives just don't get it. They seem ignorant of the vast difference between responsibility and permissiveness.

**How old are the ideas of strictness and nurturance?**
They seem to go back very, very far in history. We know, for example, that in England before the British came over to colonize America there were religious groups like the Quakers, who had a nurturant view of God, and groups like the Puritans, who had a strict father view of God. The New England colonies were mainly Puritan, though John Winthrop had a nurturant view of the colony he was establishing, and the nurturant view of God has existed side by side with the strict one in this country ever since.

In the nineteenth century, Horace Bushnell wrote about "Christian nurture." From the period of the abolitionists through the 1920s there was a lively discussion of the nurturant view of God. Moreover, students of religion have shown that there are strict and nurturant views of religion that go back as far as biblical and prebiblical times. These distinctions been there for a very, very long time.

**Does the strict father model imply that conservatives don't love their kids, and does the nurturant parent model imply that progressives don't believe in discipline?**
Not at all. In the strict father model, physically disciplining a child who has done wrong, by inflicting sufficient pain, is a form of love—"tough love." Given the duty to impose "loving discipline," lots of hugging and other loving behavior are permissible, and often recommended afterward. It's just a matter of first things first.

In the nurturant parent model, discipline arises not through painful physical punishment, but through the promotion of responsible behavior via empathetic connection, the example of responsible behavior set by the parents, the open discussion of what the parents expect (and why!), and, in the case of noncoop- eration, the removal of those privileges that go with cooperation ("Time out!" and "You're grounded."). A child raised through nuturance is a child who has achieved positive internal discipline without painful physical punishment. It is achieved through praise for cooperation, understanding the privileges that go with cooper- ation, clear guidelines, open discussion, and the example of par- ents who live by their nurturant values.

**What are the complexities of the models?**
The models, as discussed in detail in chapter 17 of *Moral Politics*, have built-in complexities.

First, just about everybody in American culture has both models, either actively or passively. For example, to understand a

John Wayne movie, you must have a strict father model in your brain, at least passively. You may not live by the model, but you can use it to understand the strict father narratives that permeate our culture. Nurturant narratives permeate our culture as well.

Second, many people use both models, but in different parts of their lives. For example, a female lawyer might be strict in the courtroom but nurturant at home.

Third, you may have been brought up badly with one model, and may have rejected it. Many liberals had miserable strict father upbringings.

Fourth, there are three natural dimensions of variation for applying a given model: an ideological/pragmatic dimension, a radical/moderate dimension, and a means/ends dimension.

Both a progressive and a conservative can be unyielding ideologues, or they may be pragmatic—willing to compromise on a proposal either for reasons of real world workability or political viability.

In addition, both progressives and conservatives can vary on the two radical/moderate scales: the amount of change and the speed of change. Thus radical conservative ideologues are unwilling to compromise, and insist on the most rapid and complete change possible.

Incidentally, the word *conservative* is not necessarily about conserving anything. It is about strict father morality. There is no contradiction in talking about "radical conservatives." Indeed, Robert Reich, in his recent book *Reason*, uses the term *radcon* to talk about radical conservatives. From this perspective a "moderate" can be either a progressive or a conservative who is pragmatic and/or wants slow change, a bit at a time. It is sometimes said that there is a third moderate model, very different from the other two, but I have not yet seen such a model proposed explicitly.

Another common variation occurs in distinguishing ends and means. There are people with progressive politics (nurturant ends) who have strict father means. These are the militant progressives.

The most extreme case is the authoritarian antiauthoritarians: those with antiauthoritarian progressive ends but authoritarian strict father organizations.

Last, there are the types—the special cases—of progressives and conservatives that we discussed in chapter 1: the socioeconomic, identity politics, environmentalist, civil libertarian, antiauthoritarian, and spiritual progressives; and the financial, social, libertarian, neocon (see chapter 7), and religious conservatives. They are all instances of the nurturant and strict models, but each restricts the form of reasoning used.

**The notion of reframing sounds manipulative. How is framing different from spin or propaganda?**

Framing is normal. Every sentence we say is framed in some way. When we say what we believe, we are using frames that we think are relatively accurate. When a conservative uses the "tax relief" frame, chances are that he or she really believes that taxation is an affliction. However, frames can also be used manipulatively. The use, for example, of "Clear Skies Act" to name an act that increases air pollution is a manipulative frame. And it's used to cover up a weakness that conservatives have, namely that the public doesn't like legislation that increases air pollution, and so they give it a name that conveys the opposite frame. That's pure manipulation.

Spin is the manipulative use of a frame. Spin is used when something embarrassing has happened or has been said, and it's an attempt to put an innocent frame on it—that is, to make the embarrassing occurrence sound normal or good.

Propaganda is another manipulative use of framing. Propaganda is an attempt to get the public to adopt a frame that is not true and is known not to be true, for the purpose of gaining or maintaining political control.

The reframing I am suggesting is neither spin nor propaganda. Progressives need to learn to communicate using frames that they really believe, frames that express what their moral views really are. I strongly recommend against any deceptive framing. I think it is not just morally reprehensible, but also impractical, because deceptive framing usually backfires sooner or later.

**Why don't progressives take advantage of wedge issues?**
Conservatives have been thinking about the strategic use of ideas and progressives haven't, but we could. We could perfectly well use wedge issues. They're all around us. Take something like clean air and clean water. Conservatives want clean air and clean water. That can be made into a wedge issue.

Imagine a campaign for poison-free communities, starting with mercury as the poison of choice, then going on to other kinds of poison in our air and in our water, around us in various forms. That could be made into an effective wedge issue, splitting the conservatives who care about their own and their children's health from those who are simply against government regulation. The very issue would create a frame in which regulation favors health, and being against regulation endangers health.

This is also a slippery slope issue. Once you get people looking at how and where mercury enters the environment—for example, from the processing of coal and many other kinds of chemicals—and you get people thinking about cleaning up mercury, and about mercury poisoning, and how it works in the environment, you can go onto the next poison in the environment, and the poison after that, and the poison after that.

This is an issue that is not just about mercury or about poisons in the environment, but about nurturant morality in general. Wedge issues are stand-ins for the whole of a moral system. Abortion is an issue that serves as a stand-in for the control of women's lives and for a moral hierarchy that conservatives want to impose. Abortion, as we have seen, is a stand-in for strict father morality in general. Similarly, there are all sorts of wedge issues that can be stand-ins for progressive morality in general.

**Is religion inherently conservative? Are progressive ideals inconsistent with religious beliefs?**

Conservatives would have us believe that religions are conservative, but they're not. Millions of Christians in this country are liberal Christians. Most Jews are liberal Jews. And I suspect that most Muslims in America are progressive, liberal Muslims, not radically conservative Muslims. However, the progressive religious community in this country is not well organized, while the conservative religious community is extremely well organized. One of the problems is that the progressive religious community, particularly progressive Christianity, doesn't really know how to express its own theology in a way that makes its politics clear, whereas conservative Christians do know the direct link between their theology and their politics. Conservative Christianity is a strict father religion. Here's how the strict father view of the world is mapped onto conservative Christianity.

First, God is understood as punitive—that is, if you sin you are going to go to hell, and if you don't sin you are going to go be rewarded. But since people tend to sin at one point or another in their lives, how is it possible for them to ever get to heaven? The answer in conservative Christianity is Christ. What Jesus does is offer them a chance to get to heaven. The idea is this: Christ suffered on the cross so much that he built up moral credit sufficient for all people, forever. He then offered a chance to get to heaven—that is, redemption—on the following terms, strict father terms: If you accept Jesus as your savior, that is, as your moral authority, and agree to follow the moral authority of your minister and your church, then you can get to heaven. But that is going to require discipline. You need to be disciplined enough to follow the rules, and if you don't, then you are going to go to hell. So Jesus, with his moral credit that he gained from suffering, can pay off your debts—that is, your sins—and allow you to get into heaven, but only if you toe the line.

Liberal Christianity is very, very different. Liberal Christianity sees God as essentially beneficent, as wanting to help people. The central idea in liberal Christianity is grace, where grace is understood as a kind of metaphorical nurturance. In liberal Christianity, you can't earn grace—you are given grace unconditionally by God unconditionally. But you have to accept grace, you have to be near God to get his grace, you can be filled with grace, you can be healed by grace, and you are made into a moral person through God's grace.

In other words, grace is metaphorical nurturance. That is, just as nurturance feeds you, heals you, takes care of you, just as a nurturant parent teaches you to be nurturant and allows you to be a moral being, just as you can't get nurturance unless you are close to your parents, just as you must accept nurturance in order to get it, so all of these things about nurturance are true of grace in liberal Christianity. Nurturance comes with unconditional love, in the case of grace, the unconditional love of God. What makes a religion nurturant is that it metaphorically views God as a nurturant parent. In a nurturant form of religion, your spiritual experience has to do with your connection to other people and the world, and your spiritual practice has to do with your service to other people and to your community. This is why nurturant Christians are progressives; because they have a nurturant morality, just as progressives have.

But at present nurturant Christians, Jews, Muslims, and Buddhists in this country are not organized. They are not seen as a single movement, a progressive religious movement. Worse, secular progressives do not see those with a nurturant form of religion as natural members of the same political movement. Not only do spiritual progressives need to unite with each other, they need to unite with secular progressives, who share the same moral system and political objectives.

**What is a strategic initiative, and how is it different from regular policy making?**
There are two kinds of strategic initiatives: The first is what I'll call a slippery slope initiative. The idea of a slippery slope initiative is to

take a first step that seems fairly straightforward, but gets into the public eye an additional frame that you want to be there. The idea is that once the first step is taken, then it is easier and often inevitable to take the next step and the next step and the next step.

For example, consider partial-birth abortion. There are virtually no such cases. The ban on partial-birth abortion applies almost nowhere. What it does is get the idea out there that abortion is a bad thing and get at least some bans on abortion. What it does is start with the most vivid and easy case to make, then go almost step by step to a total ban on abortion.

Let's take another example. It used to be the case that conservatives tried to cut social programs one by one, and then they figured out how they could cut them all at once: through tax cuts. Cutting taxes is a strategic initiative, not of the slippery slope variety but of a deeper variety, one that has wide effects across many, many areas. If you cut taxes and create a large deficit, then when any social program comes up—it could be health care for poor children, or services for paraplegics, or whatever—there won't be enough money for it. So you end up cutting social programs across the board in health, in education, in the enforcement of environmental regulations, and so on. At the same time you reward those who you see as the good people, namely the wealthy people—those who were disciplined enough to become wealthy.

There are other kinds of strategic initiatives as well. Take the example of same-sex marriage. Same-sex marriage contradicts large parts of the strict father model. If it's a lesbian marriage there's no father at all, and in a gay marriage, where there are two fathers, neither of them fits the traditional view of the male strict father. Opposing same-sex marriage is thus reinforcing and extending strict father morality itself, which is the highest calling of the conservative moral system. Same-sex marriage is therefore a stand-in; it evokes the larger issue, namely what moral system is to govern our country.

The same is true of the issue of abortion. Allowing women to decide for themselves on whether to end a pregnancy flies in the face of the whole idea of a strict father family model. In the strict father model, it is the father who decides whether his wife or daughter should have an abortion. As it is the father who controls his daughter's sexuality, when the daughter takes a lover, then the father loses control. If the father is to maintain control over his family, then the women in the family cannot freely control their own sexual behavior and their own ability to reproduce. Abortion is therefore not inherently a political issue, but only a political issue when it comes to whether strict father morality is to reign in American life. Abortion is a stand-in for the larger issue: Is strict father morality going to rule America?

**So all I have to do to reframe my issue is think up some sound bite–worthy terms and use them in place of the conservative terms?**
No! Reframing is not just about words and language. Reframing is about ideas. The ideas have to be in place in people's brains before the sound bite can make any sense. For example, take the idea of "the commons"—that is, our common inheritance, like the atmosphere or the electromagnetic spectrum (bandwidths). These are the common inheritances of all humanity, and most people who discuss them in this way refer to them as "the commons." Yet the idea of a common inheritance and of using it for the public good is not yet part of the frame structure that most people use every day. For this reason you can't just make up a sound bite about the commons and have most people understand it and agree with it.

**If Republicans have such a huge infrastructure, how do we catch up?**
Progressives know that they have to make investments in media. What they tend not to know is that they have to make investments in framing and in language. The big advantage we have is this: Whereas it took more than thirty years, billions of dollars, and forty-three institutes for conservatives to reframe public

debate so the debate occurs on their turf, we have the advantage of having science on our side. Through cognitive science and through linguistics, we know how they did it. And we know how we can do the equivalent for progressives in a much shorter time and with many fewer resources. We also know how they've done their linguistic training, and we know how to do it ourselves.

Unfortunately, many progressives think this can be done through ad agencies and through pollsters. That's a mistake. You really do need linguists and cognitive scientists.

**What is the difference between the Rockridge Institute and other progressive think tanks? Are there any other think tanks that work on framing?**
Rockridge is entirely dedicated to reframing the public debate, both from a policy perspective and from a linguistic perspective. Other progressive think tanks have other primary functions: responding to the initiatives of the right, answering conservative charges, telling the truth when there are conservative lies, and constructing specific policies that progressives can use. All of these are important functions, but they do not replace the framing function, a function that is absolutely necessary. To my knowledge, there are no other think tanks devoted to the overall framing of issues from both a policy perspective and a communicative perspective.

**I don't see much evidence of the Republican infrastructure. I can't find anything about this guy Luntz or any of the stuff he wrote. What does this infrastructure consist of, and how exactly does it work to influence discourse?**
Luntz runs a business. He trains conservatives in how to think and talk, and his manual is used as part of his business. It is therefore proprietary information and isn't available to the public. Occasionally, a copy is leaked and sent over the Internet, and that's basically how we know about it.

Most of the research at the conservative think tanks is done in private, but they all have a public face. They put out reports, their scholars write articles in well-placed journals, they write op-eds, and they write books. All of these are in the public domain, but they're not marked CONSERVATIVE INFRASTRUCTURE. It is as if lots of independent people were simply doing different things.

However, there is coordination, and their efforts are linked. The major think tanks have large media operations, round-the-clock TV and radio studios, for example. Eighty percent of the talking heads that appear on American television are conservatives, many of them from these think tanks. They have all been given extensive media training, as well as language training. In some cases half of the budget of a major institute may be dedicated to getting the ideas of that institute into the media. There are agents who get the scholars at the institute onto radio and TV shows, and who get their books published. There are writers who write press releases that can be read directly on radio and TV news programs, or put directly into a newspaper story. These releases are faxed to newspapers and radio and TV stations all over the country. Since most media outlets like radio stations and newspapers, and even small TV stations, are understaffed, they tend to use well-written press releases directly, as if they were news written up by their news staff. There's also communication—across the think tanks, the Washington political leaders, and those in the media—that coordinates the language to be used. When the same language is used by many people across the country to frame an issue, it comes to be accepted as normal because it has become part of people's brains.

**I know conservatives have deep disagreements among themselves. How do they manage to sound so consistent so often?**
Grover Norquist has a meeting every week of major conservative leaders and spokesmen, at which they air their differences on issues of the day. When there is a consensus or a majority view,

then the group tends to agree as a whole to support that consensus or majority view. If they happen to disagree with it this week, they know that next week or the week after, their views will be the consensus or majority views. Under this system everybody knows that they will win most of the time, but not all of time.

**Isn't tax relief the natural way to talk about taxes? I'm a progressive, but I have to admit, they do seem burdensome sometimes.**
Homework in school is burdensome too, but you have to do it if you're going to learn anything. Exercise is burdensome, but you have to do it if you're going to be in good physical shape. Taxes are necessary if we are going to make wise investments in our national infrastructure that will pay off for all of us years and years in the future. That includes investments in things like education and health care for those who can't afford it. Education and health care are investments in people. They are wise investments because they give us an educated citizenry, an educated workforce, and a healthy and efficient workforce. Those are the practical reasons for taxes. Other reasons for taxes are public services—like police and fire, disaster relief, and so on.

Those are the practical reasons for taxes, but there are moral reasons as well. Education and health are important factors in fulfillment in life, and this country is about fulfillment in life. There is a reason why the Declaration of Independence talks about the pursuit of happiness and links it to liberty. The reason is that they go together. Without liberty, there can be no fulfillment in life. Thus there are practical reasons why it makes sense to understand taxation as investment, and there are moral reasons to understand taxation as paying your dues in a country where you can pursue happiness because there is liberty and freedom.

**How do you respond or reply directly to a Republican strategic initiative?**
You can't, and that's why they're clever. Tax cuts are not about tax

cuts. That's why you can't reply directly to tax cuts so easily. They are about getting rid of all social programs and regulations of business. Vouchers and school testing are not ultimately about vouchers and school testing; they are about conservative control of the content of education. To respond you have to put the individual issue in a much larger framework that fits your own understanding and your understanding of the situation. Tort reform is not about tort reform; it is about allowing corporations to act without restraints, and about taking funding away from the Democratic Party, since trial lawyers are a major source of Democratic funding.

Instead of trying to reply to strategic initiatives, you need to reframe the larger issues at stake from your point of view. You can discuss the strategic initiative, or at least some parts of it, from your framework. Take tort reform. Trial lawyers are really *public protection attorneys*, and tort law is law that allows for public protection—it's public protection law. When tort law tries to cap claims and settlements, its effect is to take claims out of the hands of juries—that is, to close the courtroom door, to create closed courts instead of open courts. In open courts, where there are juries, the jury can decide whether a given claim is a matter of public protection. Large settlements often have to do with issues of public protection—that is, they go beyond the case at hand. And open courts are the last defense that the public has against unscrupulous or negligent corporations or professionals. When they talk about the lawsuits you don't just say, "No, no, the lawsuits weren't frivolous," you talk instead about public protection, about open courts, about the right to have juries decide, and about the last line of defense against unscrupulous or negligent corporations.

**If facts that don't fit frames are rejected, does that mean we should stop using facts in our arguments?**
Obviously not. Facts are all-important. They are crucial. But they must be framed appropriately if they are to be an effective part of

public discourse. We have to know what a fact has to do with moral principles and political principles. We have to frame those facts as effectively and as honestly as we can. And honest framing of the facts will entail other frames that can be checked with other facts.

**How do progressive values differ from traditional American values?** They don't differ. Progressive values *are* traditional American values, all the values we are proud of.

We are proud of the victories for equality and against hierarchy: the emancipation of the slaves, women's suffrage, the union movement, the integration of the armed forces, the civil rights movement, the woman's movement, the environmental movement, and the gay rights movement.

We are proud of FDR's conception of government "for the people" and his rally for hope against fear.

We are proud of the Marshall Plan, which helped to erase the notion of "enemies."

We are proud of John Kennedy's call to public service, of Martin Luther King's insistence on nonviolence in the face of brutality, of Cesar Chavez's ability to bring pride and organization to the worst treated of workers.

Progressive thought is as American as apple pie. Progressives want political equality, good public schools, healthy children, care for the aged, police protection, family farms, air you can breathe, water you can drink, fish in our streams, forests you can hike in, songbirds and frogs, livable cities, ethical businesses, journalists who tell the truth, music and dance, poetry and art, and jobs that pay a living wage to everyone who works.

Progressive activists—for living wages, women's rights, human rights, the environment, health, voter registration, and so on—are American patriots, working with unselfish dedication to making a better world, a world that fits fundamental American values and principles.

# How to Respond to Conservatives

The following is a letter I received while writing this chapter. It arrived several days after I had appeared on a TV show, *NOW with Bill Moyers*.

> I listened to Dr. Lakoff last Friday night on *NOW* with great interest. I love the use of words and have been consistently puzzled at how the far right has co-opted so many definitions.
>
> So I tried an experiment I wanted to tell you about. I took several examples from the interview; particularly trial vs. public protection lawyer and gay marriage and used those examples all week on AOL's political chat room. Every time someone would scream about [John] Edwards's being a trial lawyer, I'd respond with public protection lawyer and how they are the last defense against negligent corporations and [are] professional, and that the opposite of a public protection lawyer is a corporate lawyer who typically makes $400-500/per hr., and we pay that in higher prices for good and services.
>
> Every time someone started screaming about "gay marriage" I'd ask if they want the federal government to tell them who they could marry. I'd go on to explain when challenged that once government has crossed the huge barrier into telling one group of people who they could not marry, it is only a small step to telling other groups, and a smaller yet step to telling people who they had to marry.
>
> I also asked for definitions. Every time someone

would holler "dirty liberal," I'd request their definition of "liberal."

The last was my own hot button. Every time
someone would scream "abortion," "baby-killer,"
etc., I'd suggest that if they are anti-abortion, then
by all means, they should not have one.

I've got to tell you, the results were startling to
me. I had some other people (completely unknown
to me) join me and take up the same tacks. By last
night, the chat room was civil. An amazing (to me)
number of posters turned off their capitalization
and we were actually having conversations.

I'm going to keep this up, but I really wanted you
to know that I heard Dr. Lakoff, appreciate his
work, and am trying to put it into practice. And it's
really really fun.

Thanks,
Penney Kolb

This book is written for people like Penney Kolb. Progressives
are constantly put in positions where they are expected to respond
to conservative arguments. It may be over Thanksgiving dinner,
around the water cooler, or in front of an audience. But because
conservatives have commandeered so much of the language, progressives are often put on the defensive with little or nothing to
say in response.

The earlier chapters are meant to explain who conservatives
are, what they stand for, what kind of morality they see themselves
as having, and how their family values shape their politics. They
are also meant to make explicit what is usually felt but not articulated—progressive family values and how they carry over into progressive politics. And finally there is an introduction to
framing—what mistakes to avoid and how to reframe, with some
chapters providing examples of how framing works.

But sooner or later, you are in Penney's position. What do you do? Penney's instincts are impeccable, and provide us with guidelines.

- Progressive values are the best of traditional American values. Stand up for your values with dignity and strength. You are a true patriot because of your values.
- Remember that right-wing ideologues have convinced half of the country that the strict father family model, which is bad enough for raising children, should govern our national morality and politics. This is the model that the best in American values has defeated over and over again in the course of our history—from the emancipation of the slaves to women's suffrage, Social Security and Medicare, civil rights and voting rights acts, and *Brown v. the Board of Education* and *Roe v. Wade*. Each time we have unified our country more behind our finest traditional values.
- Remember that everybody has both strict and nurturant models, either actively or passively, perhaps active in different parts of their lives. Your job is to activate for politics the nurturant, progressive values already there (perhaps only passively) in your interlocutors.
- Show respect to the conservatives you are responding to. No one will listen to you if you don't accord them respect. Listen to them. You may disagree strongly with everything that is being said, but you should know what is being said. Be sincere. Avoid cheap shots. What if they don't show you respect? Two wrongs don't make a right. Turn the other cheek and show respect anyway. That takes character and dignity. Show character and dignity.
- Avoid a shouting match. Remember that the radical right requires a culture war, and shouting is the discourse form of that culture war. Civil discourse is the

discourse form of nurturant morality. You win a victory when the discourse turns civil. They win when they get you to shout.

- What if you have moral outrage? You should have moral outrage. But you can display it with controlled passion. If you lose control, they win.
- Distinguish between ordinary conservatives and nasty ideologues. Most conservatives are personally nice people, and you want to bring out their niceness and their sense of neighborliness and hospitality.
- Be calm. Calmness is a sign that you know what you are talking about.
- Be good-humored. A good-natured sense of humor shows you are comfortable with yourself.
- Hold your ground. Always be on the offense. Never go on defense. Never whine or complain. Never act like a victim. Never plead. Avoid the language of weakness, for example, rising intonations on statements. Your voice should be steady. Your body and voice should show optimism. You should convey passionate conviction without losing control.
- Conservatives have parodied liberals as weak, angry (hence not in control of their emotions), weak-minded, softhearted, unpatriotic, uninformed, and elitist. Don't give them any opportunities to stereotype you in any of these ways. Expect these stereotypes, and deal with them when they come up.
- By the way you conduct yourself, show strength, calmness, and control; an ability to reason; a sense of realism; love of country; a command of the basic facts; and a sense of being an equal, not a superior. At the very least you want your audience to think of you with respect, as someone they may disagree with but who they have to take seriously. In many situations this is

the best you can hope for. You have to recognize those situations and realize that a draw with dignity is a victory in the game of being taken seriously.

- Many conversations are ongoing. In an ongoing conversation, your job is to establish a position of respect and dignity, and then keep it.
- Don't expect to convert staunch conservatives.
- You can make considerable progress with biconceptuals, those who use both models but in different parts of their life. They are your best audience. Your job is to capture territory of the mind. With biconceptuals your goal is to find out, if you can by probing, just which parts of their life they are nurturant about. For example, ask who they care about the most, what responsibilities they feel they have to those they care about, and how they carry out those responsibilities. This should activate their nurturant models as much as possible. Then, while the nurturant model is active for them, try linking it to politics. For example, if they are nurturant at home but strict in business, talk about the home and family and how they relate to political issues. *Example:* Real family values mean that your parents, as they age, don't have to sell their home or mortgage their future to pay for health care or the medications they need.
- Avoid the usual mistakes. Remember, don't just negate the other person's claims; reframe. The facts unframed will not set you free. You cannot win just be stating the true facts and showing that they contradict your opponent's claims. Frames trump facts. His frames will stay and the facts will bounce off. Always reframe.
- If you remember nothing else about framing, remember this: *Once your frame is accepted into the discourse, everything you say is just common sense.* Why? Because that's

what common sense is: reasoning within a common-place, accepted frame.

- Never answer a question framed from your opponent's point of view. Always reframe the question to fit your values and your frames. This may make you uncomfortable, since normal discourse styles require you to directly answer questions posed. That is a trap. Practice changing frames.
- Be sincere. Use frames you really believe in, based on values you really hold.
- A useful thing to do is to use rhetorical questions: *Wouldn't it be better if . . . ?* Such a question should be chosen to presuppose your frame. *Example:* Wouldn't it be better if we had a president who went to war with a plan to secure the peace?
- Stay away from set-ups. Fox News shows and other rabidly conservative shows try to put you in an impossible situation, where a conservative host sets the frame and insists on it, where you don't control the floor, can't present your case, and are not accorded enough respect to be taken seriously. If the game is fixed, don't play.
- Tell a story. Find stories where your frame is built into the story. Build up a stock of effective stories.
- Always start with values, preferably values all Americans share like security, prosperity, opportunity, freedom, and so on. Pick the values most relevant to the frame you want to shift to. Try to win the argument at the values level. Pick a frame where your position exemplifies a value everyone holds—like fairness. *Example:* Suppose someone argues against a form of universal health care. If people don't have health care, he argues, it's their own fault. They're not working hard enough or not managing their money properly. We shouldn't have to pay for their lack of initiative or their

financial mismanagement. *Frame shift:* Most of the forty million people who can't afford health care work full-time at essential jobs that cannot pay enough to get them health care. Yet these working people support the lifestyles of the top three-quarters of our population. Some forty million people have to do those hard jobs— or you don't have your lifestyle. America promises a decent standard of living in return for hard work. These workers have *earned* their health care by doing essential jobs to support the economy. There is money in the economy to pay them. Tax credits are the easiest mechanism. Their health care would be covered by having the top 2 percent pay the same taxes they used to pay. It's only *fair* that the wealthy pay for their own lifestyles, and that people who provide those lifestyles get paid fairly for it.

• Be prepared. You should be able to recognize the basic frames that conservatives use, and you should prepare frames to shift to. The Rockridge Institute Web site (www.rockridgeinstitute.org) posts nonpartisan analyses of frame shifting. *Example:* A tax cut proponent says, We should get rid of taxes. People know how to spend their money better than the government. *Reframe:* The government has made very wise investments with taxpayer money. Our interstate highway system, for example. You couldn't build a highway with your tax refund. The government built them. Or the Internet, paid for by taxpayer investment. You could not make your own Internet. Most of our scientific advances have been made through funding from the National Science Foundation and the National Institute of Health— great government investments of taxpayer money. No matter how wisely you spent your own money, you'd never get those scientific and medical breakthroughs.

And how far would you get hiring your own army with
your tax refund?

- Use wedge issues, cases where your opponent will violate some belief he holds no matter what he says.
*Example*: Suppose he brings up abortion. Raise the issue
of military rape treatment. Women soldiers who are
raped (by our own soldiers, in Iraq, or on military bases)
and who subsequently get pregnant presently cannot
end their pregnancies in a military hospital, because
abortions are not permitted there. A Military Rape
Treatment Act would allow our raped women soldiers
to be treated in military hospitals to end their rape-
induced pregnancies. *The wedge*: If he agrees, he sanctions abortion, in government-supported facilities no
less, where doctors would have to be trained and facilities provided for terminating pregnancies. If he dis-
agrees, he dishonors our women soldiers who are
putting their lives on the line for him. To the women it
is like being raped twice—once by a criminal soldier
and once by a self-righteous conservative.

- An opponent may be disingenuous if his real goal isn't
what he says his goal is. Politely point out the real goal,
then reframe. *Example*: Suppose he starts touting smaller
government. Point out that conservatives don't really
want smaller government. They don't want to eliminate
the military, or the FBI, or the Treasury and Commerce
Departments, or the nine-tenths of the courts that support corporate law. It is big government that they like.
What they really want to do away with is social programs—programs that invest in people, to help people to
help themselves. Such a position contradicts the values
the country was founded on—the idea of a community
where people pull together to help each other. From
John Winthrop on, that is what our nation has stood for.

- Your opponent may use language that means the opposite of what he says, called Orwellian language. Realize that he is weak on this issue. Use language that accurately describes what he's talking about to frame the discussion your way. *Example:* Suppose he cites the "Healthy Forests Initiative" as a balanced approach to the environment. Point out that it should be called "No Tree Left Behind" because it permits and promotes clear-cutting, which is destructive to forests and other living things in the forest habitat. Use the name to point out that the public likes forests, doesn't want them clear-cut, and that the use of the phony name shows weakness on the issue. Most people want to preserve the grandeur of America, not destroy it.

- Remember once more that our goal is to unite our country behind our values, the best of traditional American values. Right-wing ideologues need to divide our country via a nasty cultural civil war. They need discord and shouting and name-calling and put-downs. We win with civil discourse and respectful cooperative conversation. Why? Because it is an instance of the nurturant model at the level of communication, and our job is to evoke and maintain the nurturant model.

Those are a lot of guidelines. But there are only four really important ones:

**Show respect**
**Respond by reframing**
**Think and talk at the level of values**
**Say what you believe**

## ACKNOWLEDGMENTS

Each morning, my wife Kathleen Frumkin gets to the morning paper before I do and homes in unerringly on the greatest political outrages of the day. Much of what appears in this book is a response to those outrages and to her insights.

Pamela Morgan edited the talk that appears as chapter 1. She has also helped me work through many of the issues discussed throughout.

Don Hazen, editor of AlterNet, had the idea for this volume and did a great deal to make it possible. He has been a constant source of important questions and of help, intellectual and otherwise, in many ways.

Many of the ideas discussed here arose in discussions with David Brodwin, Jason Patent, Dan Kurtz, Katherine Allen, Alyssa Wulf, Larry Wallack, Fred Block, Carole Joffe, Jerome Karabel, Kristen Luker, Troy Duster, Ruth Rosen, Jessica DiCamillo, Melinda Franco, Jonathan Frank, Cathy Lenz, Jodi Short, and Jessica Stites.

Peter Teague of the Nathan Cummings Foundation has been an invaluable sounding board and source of ideas.

Other friends who have contributed ideas in discussions include George Akerlof, Paul Baer, Peter Barnes, Joan Blades, Wes Boyd, David Fenton, Tony Fazio, Paul Hawken, Arianna Huffington, Anne Lipow, Ted Nordhaus, Geoff Nunberg, Karen Paget, Robert Reich, Lee Rosenberg, Jon Rowe, Michael Shellenberger, Steve Silberstein, Daniel Silverman, Glenn Smith, George Soros, Alex Steffen, Deborah Tannen, Adam Werbach, Lisa Witter, Rebecca Wodder, and Richard Yanowitch.

And finally, a toast to the Father of Frame Semantics, my Berkeley colleague, Charles Fillmore.

# ABOUT THE AUTHOR

**George Lakoff** is Richard and Rhoda Goldman Professor of Cognitive Science and Linguistics at the University of California, Berkeley, and is a founding senior fellow at the Rockridge Institute.* He is one of the world's best-known linguists. His expertise is in cognitive linguistics, the scientific study of the nature of thought and its expression in language.

Since the mid-1980s he has been applying cognitive linguistics to the study of politics, especially the framing of public political debate. He is the author of the influential book, *Moral Politics: How Liberals and Conservatives Think* (second edition, 2002). Since 2002, he has consulted with the leaders of hundreds of advocacy groups on framing issues, lectured to large audiences across the country, run dozens of workshops for activists, spoken regularly on radio talk shows and TV shows, spoken twice at the Democratic Senators' Policy Retreat, consulted with progressive pollsters and advertising agencies, been interviewed at length in the public media, served as a consultant in major political campaigns, and done extensive research for Rockridge.

In addition to his work on political thought and language, he has been active in his academic discipline. He has lectured at major universities in dozens of countries around the world. He is currently on the Science Board of the Santa Fe Institute (1995–2001), has served as president of the International Cognitive Linguistics Association and on the Governing Board of the Cognitive Science Society, and is co-director with Jerome Feldman of the Neural Theory of Language Project at the International Computer Science Institute at Berkeley.

He is the author of *Women, Fire, and Dangerous Things: What*

---

*Affiliation appears for identification purposes only. The Rockridge Institute, a non-partisan tax-exempt 501(c)(3) research and educational institution, does not endorse or oppose any candidate for elected office or any political party. Views expressed in this book are those of the author and not necessarily those of the Institute.

*Categories Reveal About The Mind* (1987) and coauthor of
*Metaphors We Live By* (1980, 2003) [with Mark Johnson], *More
Than Cool Reason* (1989) [with Mark Turner], *Philosophy in the
Flesh: The Embodied Mind and Its Challenge To The Western
Tradition* (1999) [with Mark Johnson], and *Where Mathematics
Comes From: How the Embodied Mind Brings Mathematics Into Being*
(2000) [with Rafael Núñez].

Chelsea Green is committed to being a sustainable business enterprise as well as a publisher of books on the politics and practice of
sustainability. This means reducing natural resource and energy
use to the maximum extent possible. We print our books and cat-
alogs on chlorine-free recycled paper, using soy-based inks, whenever possible. *Don't Think of an Elephant!* was printed on Legacy
Trade Book Natural, a 100 percent post-consumer waste recycled,
old growth forest-free paper supplied by Webcom.

the politics and practice of sustainable living

Chelsea Green has introduced a new series called "Politics of the Living," a collection of hard-hitting works by major writers exposing the global governmental and corporate assault on life.

For twenty years Chelsea Green has published the best books on green building, renewable energy, organic gardening and sustainable agriculture, permaculture, and eco-food. Our series of Slow Food City Guides includes *The Slow Food Guide to New York City* and *The Slow Food Guide to Chicago*, produced in partnership with Slow Food USA.

For more information about Chelsea Green, or to request a free catalog, call toll-free (800) 639-4099, or write to us at P.O. Box 428, White River Junction, Vermont 05001. Visit our Web site at www.chelseagreen.com.

*Strangely Like War: The Global Assault on Forests*
Derrick Jensen &
George Draffan
ISBN 1-931498-45-8
$15.00

*Limits to Growth: The 30-Year Update*
Donella Meadows,
Jorgen Randers,
Dennis Meadows
ISBN 1-931498-58-X
$22.50

*Guantánamo: What the World Should Know*
Michael Ratner &
Ellen Ray
ISBN 1-931498-64-4
$15.00

*High Noon for Natural Gas: The New Energy Crisis*
Julian Darley
ISBN 1-931498-53-9
$18.00

# CHELSEA GREEN
## PUBLISHING

the politics and practice of sustainable living

SUSTAINABLE LIVING has many facets. Chelsea Green's celebration of the sustainable arts has led us to publish trend-setting books about innovative building techniques, regenerative forestry, organic gardening and agriculture, solar electricity and renewable energy, local and bioregional democracy, and whole foods and Slow food.

For more information about Chelsea Green, visit our Web site at www.chelseagreen.com, where you will find more than 200 books on the politics and practice of sustainable living.

## Shelter

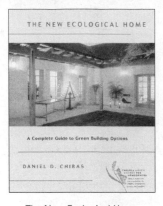

The New Ecological Home:
A Complete Guide to
Green Building Options
Daniel D. Chiras
ISBN 1-931498-16-4
$35.00

## Planet

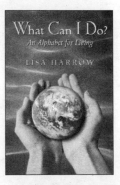

What Can I Do?
An Alphabet for Living
Lisa Harrow
ISBN 1-931498-66-0
$7.95

## People

This Organic Life:
Confessions of a Suburban
Homesteader
Joan Dye Gussow
ISBN 1-931498-24-5
$16.95

## Food

The Slow Food Guide to
New York City:
Restaurants, Markets, Bars
Patrick Martins &
Ben Watson
ISBN 1-931498-27-X
$20.00